AT THE
OASIS

Bill McDonald

Note for Librarians: A cataloguing record for this book is available from Library and Archives
Canada at www.collectionscanada.ca/amicus/index-e.html
ISBN 1-4120-6810-X

*Printed in Victoria, BC, Canada. Printed on paper with minimum 30% recycled fibre. Trafford's print shop
runs on "green energy" from solar, wind and other environmentally-friendly power sources.*

TRAFFORD
PUBLISHING™
Offices in Canada, USA, Ireland and UK
This book was published *on-demand* in cooperation with Trafford Publishing. On-demand
publishing is a unique process and service of making a book available for retail sale to the
public taking advantage of on-demand manufacturing and Internet marketing. On-demand
publishing includes promotions, retail sales, manufacturing, order fulfilment, accounting and
collecting royalties on behalf of the author.

Book sales for North America and international:
Trafford Publishing, 6E–2333 Government St.,
Victoria, BC v8t 4p4 CANADA
phone 250 383 6864 (toll-free 1 888 232 4444)
fax 250 383 6804; email to orders@trafford.com
Book sales in Europe:
Trafford Publishing (uk) Limited, 9 Park End Street, 2nd Floor
Oxford, UK ox1 1hh UNITED KINGDOM
phone 44 (0)1865 722 113 (local rate 0845 230 9601)
facsimile 44 (0)1865 722 868; info.uk@trafford.com
Order online at:
trafford.com/05-1721
10 9 8 7 6 5 4 3 2 1

ACKNOWLEDGEMENTS

"**A Sistine Chapel of My Own**" was originally published in *RE:AL The Journal of Liberal Arts*, Volume XXVII, Numbers 1 & 2, SPRING/FALL 2002.

"**Holy Water**" wasoriginally published in *Poet Lore*, Volume 96, No. 3, Fall 2001.

"**A Cosmic Villanelle**" was originally published in *Artword Quarterly*, Fall 1999, No. 18, and was nominated by them for the Pushcart Prize XXV Anthology.

"**A Private Goodbye**" was originally published in *The Portland Review*, Volume 49, Number 1, FALL/WINTER 2001.

"**A Dangerous Idea**" was originally published in *Minnesota Literature*, Volume 28, Number 4, December, 2002. It was also the first place winner of that year's Minnesota Literature Essay Contest.

"**Trees, By God**" has been accepted for publication by *The North Dakota Quarterly*.

Cover photo is by ***RONVANZEE*** Photography, Bayport, Minnesota

CONTENTS

Author's Preface

As I look back at eighty I find that I have many stories to tell, and I search for the best ways to tell them. In one way, I feel a kinship with Emily Dickinson—a sense that this book is my letter to a world that never wrote to me, and that my life would have been easier if someone had just told me some of this stuff a long time ago. In another way though, it seems as if the world has been writing to me all along—writing and writing, writing and repeating until her slow-witted student finally begins to understand bits and pieces of what she has been saying. And then I am grateful for having lived this long.

But it also occurs to me that I had this same thought at age fifty—and at sixty—and at seventy. On my fiftieth birthday I remember (*Ah, distinctly I remember*) thinking about how good it was to be able to finally understand the world and to be comfortable with my place in it. It was a huge relief to have the stupidity of my youth behind me. But then at sixty I realized that these things had just then happened, and I was nonplussed to imagine how I could have thought them to be true when I was but a callow fifty.

So, as such thoughts recur again at eighty, these thoughts about the world and my supposedly improved mastery of my place in it, I am more cautious about them. But still, I have these stories to tell. Not stories, exactly—not made up stories—but things that have happened to me, and to others, and to the world—and ideas about those happenings. The ideas come partly from me and partly from others—from literature, from friends, even from politicians.

Not made up stories, I say, but there are a few minor exceptions, and I need to explain them. It has to do with the search for the best way to tell my stories. Herodotus, the ancient Greek historian, had the same problem when he was writing about the history of events before his time. The episode that is exactly right to properly convey the correct impression of the whole is often elusive; it is hard to find a truly representative example. Herodotus argued that the historian was entitled, even obligated, to create his own episode.

"Very few things happen at the right time, and the rest do not happen at all," he said. "The conscientious historian will correct these defects."

Modern historians do not feel so free, nor do I, but there are situations where a complete account would only bore the reader for no good purpose—where literary necessity demands shortcuts. Dialog is an example. It is almost impossible to repeat dialog exactly as it occurred. Writing is not speaking; real people talk partly in grunts and grimaces, with mumbles and hand waving and hems and haws. To get it all on paper as it was actually said would not only challenge the writer mightily, it would also bore the reader to tears.

There are other accepted departures from fact as well. Mike Royko, the noted Chicago Tribune columnist, often referred to his conversations with Slats Grobnik, and quoted Slats at length. But his readers understood that Slats was simply a literary device—they didn't demand, except with tongue in cheek, that Mike produce him. They assumed, without being told, that there was no such person as Slats Grobnik

In my case, my ventures away from strict fact are associated with conversations at the Oasis Café, a place where the concept of truth is known to be somewhat relative in the first place. I use these conversations partly to introduce other topics—other essays. As a result, these pieces about conversations at the Oasis, although they comprise only a small part of the book, provide something of a unifying theme—a through narrative that connects disparate topics. Like Herodotus, I find that I sometimes have to massage these conversations a little bit to make them fit this purpose—not much, but a little bit. I'll explain some of these diversions in more detail below. With this disclosure, I hope my reader will accept them as a legitimate literary device, as it seems to me they are.

The Oasis Café itself is very real. My home town of Stillwater, Minnesota is a border town—the St. Croix River separates it from Wisconsin. Heading south from downtown,

Highway 95 snakes its way for half a mile along a narrow ledge between a bluff on the right and the river and a railroad track on the left below, so there are no buildings except in one spot where the bluff recedes from the road briefly, leaving room for a small parking lot and the building that houses the Oasis Café. The restaurant building was constructed during the 1950s, and once sported gas pumps out in front. This was a time when gas stations came complete with attendants who greeted you, filled your tank, cleaned your windshield, checked your oil, and·took your money. I remember that Jerry McGarry pumped gas at the Oasis before he went to Vietnam and was killed.

The gas pumps are long gone, but the Oasis is little changed otherwise. It's a small place with two counters and some booths, arranged so that each waitress can serve both her counter and her booths from a narrow aisle between them. In deference to modern sensibilities, one counter has been designated "nonsmoking."

The lunch counter is passé in modern restaurants, and even the booths and tables are arranged in such a way as to assure the customers of privacy. At the Oasis, however, and at other restaurants of its era—whether by design or circumstance—going in to eat is a social experience, even if you're alone. Every customer can see almost all of the other customers and can converse with many of them without leaving his or her seat, so there is a continuous banter in which the waitress, and even the busboy, often plays a major role.

So the Oasis draws regulars, especially for breakfast—many of them are old men who sit around and discuss the vagaries of the world, both in its weightier aspects and in its trivialities. One topic that often draws our attention is the eating habits of other customers, especially their penchant for ordering a huge plate of food and then eating only a small part of it while the rest is consigned to the garbage. There is some difference of opinion about the underlying reason for this strange behavior. The most popular idea is that it simply arises from the fact that these people did not grow up during the depression. A competing theory is that younger generations have a peculiar need to show everybody that they can afford to waste stuff—even when they actually can not. Such ostentation doesn't sit well with the regulars, and they take pains to avoid any hint of it in themselves. Of two men in

4 – At the Oasis

conversation on adjoining stools, the one who has just sold off some building lots at a quarter of a million apiece will be indistinguishable from his companion who is barely making it on social security. They are in training, I like to think, for a coming day when their gravestones in the cemetery will be equally egalitarian.

I often wonder how those people, the subjects of our scrutiny, would react if they knew that their eating habits were being dissected in such merciless detail. For the regulars, their normal breakfast order is for two eggs, toast, and coffee, and when they finish and Kenny, the "busboy" (I suppose he's fifty), picks up their plates, those plates are as slick and clean as if licked by the cat.

As to the people who populate my stories about the Oasis here in this book, they are equally real, even if some of them may sometimes masquerade under false names. There is, I must confess, one exception—the character of Art Schmidt, who appears in "I Think He Died Last Year," is fictional. I had the need for a dead man whose death I could discuss lightly, and I was reluctant to use a real person out of respect for his memory and for fear of offending surviving friends and relatives, so I invented Art. I can't see that any vast, eternal plan is foiled by using this little fib for a good purpose, but I want to be up front about it. If there had been such a person as Art, our Oasis discussion of his life and death would have gone as reported, so there is still much truth in the anecdote.

In another chapter, "Art is Where You Find It," I report on a conversation I once had with Bobby Anderson. Now certainly Bobby is a real person, a man I have known well for nearly fifty years. And my account of our conversation is as accurate as I could recall it—as accurate as I would be able to recall any conversation after a lapse of years, and, undoubtedly, more accurate than I could recall most in that this one made a deep impression on me. Even so, my report does include one major departure from truth. The conversation I report took place, not at the Oasis Café, but at the local VFW. In fact I don't remember ever even seeing Bobby Anderson at the Oasis Café in all of the years I have known him.

So what prompts such manipulation of minor facts? I suppose it is simply that I want to make it easier for the reader to stay focused on the story I am trying to tell—to simplify the frame of the story without interfering with it in any essential way. It just seems better to do it that way.

Frank McCourt tells us that one day when he was in his hometown in Ireland, signing copies of *Angela's Ashes* as part of a book tour, a boyhood acquaintance came up to him to complain that Frank had, in the book, given him a nonexistent sister. Frank agreed, said that he knew perfectly well that there was no such sister, added that, at this point, even he had no idea what had ever prompted him to say such a thing, and offered the man a free copy of the book. The man's answer was classic Ireland. I like to picture him as hefting the book in his hand and answering with all of the gravitas of Ted Turner selling a billion dollar company to Steve Case:

"With the book, Frankie, we'll be forgetting about the sister," he said.

America

As early as Beowulf,
the Germans had a word for it.
They always have, it seems.
Amalric was a Goth.
Amal for a man of great or laborious enterprises
and Ric (now Reich) for something akin to power.
They expected a lot of their kings in those days.
When the Goths went south and sacked Rome
the name came too.

But the Italian tongue
wouldn't fit around double consonants.

Italians like music and rhyme in their speech.
Amalric became Amelrico, then Amerrico,
and then Amerigo, as in Amerigo Vespucci,
the Florentine explorer who followed Columbus
to the New World.

But the Germans had the last word,
as well as the first.
Waldseemuller, the mapmaker,
a Vespucci fan,
christened the New World America.
A word with a northern taste
associated with many men
before Columbus or Vespucci .

Sam

"Do I have to eat my god damn pancakes with a spoon?"

Kim rushed over in mock alarm to get Sam a fork, while everybody else chuckled. It is an old game in which Sam plays his part to the hilt, never dropping out of character. But he leaves a dollar bill on the counter as a tip—or maybe it's more like stool rent. He comes in to the Oasis Cafe before eight every morning, and sits sipping coffee and grousing to whoever has the next stool for an hour or more before he even orders his breakfast, so it's hard to imagine that there's really any hurry about his fork.

On one day about every six weeks, Sam comes in a little late. That's because of his doctor appointment. Sam is eighty-one, and has the "god damn shakes." I suppose that's what he goes to the doctor about. He's always at the clinic when they open, and is usually "outta there," and on his stool at the Oasis by eight-thirty. He is one of a group of grumpy old men who monopolize the seats along the counter in the smoking section each morning. We talk so much, and I know them so well, that I'm not always sure if I'm remembering something that they actually said, or only something I know they would have said if the proper occasion had arisen.

But Sam, even more than the others, also seems to think that terrorizing the waitresses is one of his duties in life. He demands service for himself, and even intercedes for others. On occasion I have chanced to sit next to him when the waitress was busy and didn't get to me right away. Each time, Sam soon exploded in indignation. "God," he would say. "What in the hell do they think you're sitting there for? WAITRESS!"

But Renee and Kim, who habitually serve that counter, are not easily terrorized. Both are excellent waitresses—fast and skillful, friendly and pleasant. For regular breakfast customers like me, the ordering process consists of little more than a questioning look and a responding nod. My usual coffee and wheat toast is then before me almost before I can even exchange pleasantries with my neighbors. The girls (I suppose they're forty) normally treat Sam's outbursts as some sort of an "in" joke, and make a play of scurrying to accommodate him. But sometimes, if they are especially rushed with customers in the other room, they may respond with an impatient, angry look. Then Sam will subside, although he seems to do so only with a little inward smile.

When Joy is on duty, the routine is different. Joy is an owner, or the owner's wife, I'm not sure which, and she sometimes doubles as waitress. She is not as good at it as Kim and Renee are, and she is also inclined to be a little more haughty. Kim and Renee both seem to have eyes in the back of their heads when it comes to keeping the coffee cups full, but Joy is oblivious to empty cups. Even so, Sam doesn't harass Joy. He grumbles under his breath about her, and mumbles about going to a different damn restaurant, but he never does. I don't know how much of a tip he leaves Joy.

One day in September, I seem to remember, Sam was sitting next to me and we were talking about my former neighbor, Jim, dead now, who Sam used to visit often. Jim lived opposite me, across a small lake surrounded by woods, so Sam was familiar with the area. I had nearly stumbled over a wild turkey hidden in the grass while I was walking there the previous day, and I was telling him about it. The turkey had taken flight like a pheasant would, with a speed that astonished me, given its size, and with a thunderous noise reminiscent of a 747 leaving the runway. The incident had startled me out of my wits, and had left me with a great feeling about Mother Nature and her creations, so I was enthusiastically relating my experience to Sam.

"Yeah," he said. "Well, don't sit too close to me. I suppose you're crawling with those damn wood ticks from down there."

"Ah, Sam," I said, "You city folks are too squeamish. A few wood ticks won't hurt you none. In fact, if you look at one close, they're almost beautiful. Shiny and hard and rounded off like a button, and with those nice brown on black markings."

"Bullshit," he replied, his jowls shaking. "You don't need to tell me nothing about wood ticks. Back before the war we used to hunt all of that land out there for miles around, and at all times of the year. I've pulled more damn wood ticks off of myself than I could ever count, and I don't need any more.

"Beautiful my ass," he added, shaking his fork at me. The fork held a small slab of white toast upon which he had precariously perched a piece of fried egg, so I drew back.

"Well, anyway," I finally managed, "It's the middle of September, and as you must know, by this time of the year the wood ticks are all dead. So you don't need to worry."

"Yeah, I suppose that's right," he said, returning to his breakfast. "Time seems to go so damn fast now."

Conversation With Julius Caesar

Hey, Jule! How they hittin' kid?
Just thought I'd swing by. Chew the fat,
bring you the news, and like that.
It's been a while.

First off, you oughta know
you've not been forgotten.
More people know your name now
than when you were hackin' up Gaul.

And the way you were born--
You know, with the knife? Back there in Spain?
Now it's an operation that goes by your name.
Cesarean section.

Another day, another guy with your same initials
mentioned your name. Prominently.

He up and divided the world
between you and him.
Render unto Caesar, he said,
those things that are Caesar's.

Sort of a closed loop he made there.
Self-referential I suppose.
Deep, anyway.
Levels of abstraction–shit like that.
You might want to think on it.

Been good talkin'.
Beware the Ides and all that.
My best to Cleo if you see her.
Chow, Jule.

Tick Talk

Am I a tyrant—a torturer, an unfeeling despot? The thought plagued me as I picked a crawling wood tick off the back of my neck, stuck it onto a little piece of scotch tape, and folded the tape over, sticky side to sticky side, sealing the living tick into a cellophane tomb. I thought of Poe's character, Montresor, in "A Cask of Amontillado", as he used rocks and mortar to seal a chained and pleading Fortunato into a tiny recess in one of the vaults in the nitre-encrusted catacombs beneath his Italian castle. I did not share Montresor's maniacal glee, nor his smugness as he reflected that his erstwhile friend was undoubtedly still there, undisturbed, and that fifty long years had passed. But I did feel an uneasy kinship with him as I contemplated the tick and her situation. She was completely immobilized; even her eight tiny legs were individually encased and frozen into place—the ultimate experience in claustrophobia. She couldn't even wiggle, and she was doomed to spend the rest of her life there.

I had killed wood ticks before, but not so easily. The toughness of these small, hard, wafer-like relatives of scorpions, mites and spiders is legendary. It is almost impossible to crush one, short of using a hammer and an anvil, and the woods and fields where I work are infested with millions of them during May, June, and July. By September they are all dead, but during the earlier part of the summer they get on my body as I brush against the leaves and grass, and then, left to their own devices, crawl to some spot of their liking, dig in, and engorge themselves with my blood. The problem is to find them, pull them off (preferably before they dig in), and dispose of them. More often than not, the tick reveals her presence by causing a very slight tingle as she crawls along my skin, something noticeable only when I am in comparative repose. I usually find ticks, one after another, while I am seated in my easy chair, reading the evening paper. Some varieties of ticks carry diseases that are deadly to humans and other animals. The wood ticks in our neighborhood do not, although once they dig in, they do leave an itching welt that persists for days.

My war on wood ticks had employed a variety of weapons before I came upon the scotch tape idea several years ago. After brute force failed, I moved on to fingernail clippers, which are usually within reach and allow me to dispose of the tick without getting up out of my chair or losing my train of thought about the article I'm reading. And nail clippers are actually quite effective, although it is hard to hold the tick between the thumb and forefinger with enough of her body exposed so that it can be reached by the clipper jaws. Another recommended technique is to keep small bottles or vials of rubbing alcohol around, and to remove the cap and plop the tick in when it is found. I still find these small, sealed bottles around the house from time to time, relics of bygone years, still partly filled with alcohol and holding the embalmed bodies of dozens of wood ticks. I should have labeled those containers with the year. If I had, I could now hold the bottle up to the light and surrender myself to nostalgia— "Ah, yes. Nineteen eighty-two. A very good year."

Alcohol and nail clippers both bring quick death to the tick, but for convenience, neither can compare to the ubiquitous scotch tape. It is almost always close to hand, it is helpful for catching the tick (by plucking it from a surface), and it is convenient to dispose of. Once the tick is folded within, the tape can be thrown away like any scrap of paper.

But what of the poor tick inside? She was, in a sense, my enemy, but I have no desire to avenge myself with torture. How long does she remain in this utterly immobilized state of captivity before she dies, and does it bother her as it would you or me? As to life expectancy, my first reaction was that she might survive for weeks or months. Adult ticks eat only one meal per lifetime, so they are used to going for long periods without food. And I know from experience that a tick will often get on an item of my clothing, such as a hat or jacket, and stay there for days if the jacket is not worn again during that time. But then she re-emerges (gleefully, it always seems to me) the next time I don that jacket, and unless I am vigilant, I am apt to find her burrowed into the skin of my armpit, feasting on her sanguine meal, and creating an itching welt to remind me, for days afterward, of our earlier intimacy.

So I knew that a tick could live for a long time without much interaction with its environment, and it seemed to me that I might be doing something unspeakably cruel—dooming the poor creature to a long life of utter immobility—the ultimate torture. I felt like a fiend. Little boys who turpentine cats and pull the wings off butterflies seemed benign by comparison. Still, reluctant as I was at first to employ the deadly tape method, the convenience of it eventually won me over.

Later, perhaps in an effort to rationalize my ruthless behavior, I came to the idea that she might not live so long in there after all. Even a tick needs oxygen, I assume, and the amount of air trapped in there with the encapsulated tick must be miniscule indeed. She would deplete those few micrograms of oxygen after only a few minutes, and expire peacefully. So I felt better. Our ability to rationalize about the death and suffering of others is remarkable.

But, as the years went on, my misgivings persisted. Would she really use up the oxygen? Or would she pass into some dormant state where her life processes slowed to a virtual stop? Forms of life much higher than these arachnids are capable of protecting themselves against extreme conditions—against cold by hibernation or against arid situations by estivation. Even mammals, such as the artic ground squirrel, can live in a state of torpor where their body temperature falls to near freezing. Many die in the process, it is true, but most do not. Some snails have been revived after five years of dormancy. Many bats, mosquitoes, frogs and snakes live through the winter this way. In preparation for estivation, some lungfish even secrete slimy mucus around themselves which hardens into a tight, cocoon-like structure. Some snails seal off their breathing aperture by secreting a membrane over it, leaving a minute hole which admits the tiny amount of oxygen they need while in this state. But the most extreme examples of dormant life are seeds and spores, which have been known to survive for thousands of years.

With examples before me that ranged from life forms as primitive as a spore to those as complex as a mammal, how could I be sure that my wood tick would not also adapt to the position in which I had so ruthlessly placed her?

14 – At the Oasis

Eventually, after years of recurrent agony over this moral dilemma, I did what I should have done earlier—I sought professional help. Not from psychiatrists, no. They would have thought I was crazy. Instead, I went to some industrial scientists who I used to work with and knew well. Industry devotes a lot of scientific effort to mundane questions, even to such things as the shape of a bar of soap. Whatever sells is important to industry, so industrial scientists are used to oddball questions, and are very good at finding the answers to them.

One of these guys, true scientist that he was, grew impatient with my speculations and suggested an experimental approach. Instead of putting the tick between two pieces of tape, he said, tape it down onto a piece of glass and watch it. See how long it struggles and when it dies.

His idea didn't really work because the tape so immobilized the tick that she ceased struggling immediately, as far as I could see. Still, I thought, perhaps she was struggling inwardly but unable to produce any perceptible movement.

But this idea led me to another. I taped a tick down onto a piece of glass, immobilizing her immediately, and then left the glass on my desktop for three whole days, examining it from time to time and finding no sign of any sort of movement or other visible change in the tick.

Then I pulled the tape (and the tick) off the glass, and used the point of a needle to gently and carefully pry her loose from the sticky tape, one leg at a time, until she finally dropped free of the tape onto my desktop.

To my astonishment, she immediately righted herself and marched away. I sat there with my mouth open and watched her go, too surprised to do anything about it—or judging, perhaps, that she had earned her freedom. I don't know where she went.

This story needs a postscript, which I am unable to supply. I have temporarily put aside the moral question in favor of the physical one. I envision an experiment where twenty ticks are taped to twenty pieces of glass, and then released after various periods of time. But September has come and the ticks have gone. The physical question will have to wait for another summer, and the moral one will have to wait still longer.

Art is Where You Find It

It was early afternoon on a Wednesday. I had missed lunch, so I decided to swing by the Oasis for a bowl of soup. It seemed unusual to be walking in at that time of the day. All of the familiar faces that haunted the counter and the booths at breakfast time were missing. In fact, the place was nearly empty.

But I saw Bobby Anderson sitting on one of the stools at the no smoking counter, so I slid in next to him. "Hey," he said. "Long time, no see."

He was right about that; it must have been several years. "How's it going?" I asked. "How's Clarice?"

"Oh, she's fine—ornery as ever."

They had been neighbors when we lived in Dutchtown back in the fifties, and we had run into each other and talked like this from time to time in the years since, usually at the VFW. They still lived in Dutchtown and had, I think, grown up there. Bobby was a Navy vet from WWII, and I remember that his uniform still fit him well when he wore it to a *Come in Uniform* dance in the seventies or eighties. He could probably still get it on. He worked in Stillwater at the shoe factory for many years, but then it went out of business and he got a job working in the boiler room with Len Feeley at the 3M Main Plant in St. Paul.

"Where ya been keepin yourself?" I asked. "I never see you around town since you retired. Thought maybe you'd moved off to Florida or someplace."

"Nah, we're still in the same house. Spend quite a bit of time on the river. There's no use hanging around town—nobody left that we know anymore."

16 – At the Oasis

I let that go and searched around in my mind for a different subject. He was argumentative anyway, and both he and Clarice were "Old Stillwater" and still saw me as somewhat of a usurper, even though I had lived here for more than fifty years and my family had been here for a hundred and fifty. And they were right, too. People who grow up together as kids and continue to know each other well as adults do have a special bond—they know each other in ways that others never can.

Stillwater, once a historic, prosperous, lumbering center, had dwindled to an economically hard-pressed small town by the time Clarice and Bobby were born, but in their experience it was a great place to grow up. The historical connections were still there, the river was there, everybody knew everybody, and they lived and worked and played together. Bobby had known men like John Runk, the photographer whose historic pictures of lumberjacks and logs, the river and the town, now grace every museum and regional history book. And the outdoor world of trees, rocks, streams, animals and birds was all around him, unregulated, free to be explored and used, and his in a way that was no longer possible.

But the town, in their lifetime, had changed again. Now it was a combination of a bedroom community and a tourist trap. The businesses had left Main Street to be replaced by antique shops and fancy restaurants patronized by visitors from Minneapolis. Nobody native went downtown anymore. And the old city was surrounded by endless acres of new housing peopled by strangers who hardly even knew they lived in Stillwater.

"So," I said, "how's your goose story coming along? Did you ever write any more about it? I was waiting for that goddam gander to really raise hell in New Orleans."

He laughed, but I could see that he was pleased. "You remember that, huh? No, I never finished it—don't suppose I ever will. I think about it once in a while, though." A reminiscent grin spread over his face as the memory returned in force.

Bobby was, is, in many ways, a sort of a Minnesota Redneck, so I was surprised when I found him to be one of the few people around that were interested in my writing—not so much in the writing itself as in the fact that I was doing it—he was interested in the experience of writing. As we talked, I came to realize why. It was because he had a secret world too. It was a whimsical world where fantastic things happened in an ordinary context, and he had an occasional urge to reveal this world to others. Most people at the VFW weren't really interested, or might look askance upon such a revelation, so I think he mostly carried this secret world around inside himself. And I think that, perhaps subconsciously, he saw in me a chance to bring his story to the world, or at least to a small part of it.

I don't remember all the details of his goose story anymore, but a couple of things stood out. The first was that you had to know something about geese, which Bobby very obviously did, to appreciate the story. In spite of their tiny brains, geese have some remarkably human characteristics. There must be some common little strand of DNA that has persisted in both species ever since they diverged on the tree of life a hundred million years ago. The head gander on the pond, marshalling his troops for the trip south, looks and acts, for all the world, like an army First Sergeant haranguing his troops to ready them for a major training exercise. A pair of geese with their goslings, marching so pompously from one pond to another, is a perfect caricature of old-time parents with their brood in the Easter Parade. Geese, like humans, fairly ooze self-importance. And they do accomplish remarkable things in their long migrations, their foraging, and the raising of their families.

Bobby's goose was somewhat of a loner, just a gander and his mate, if I recall correctly, who were flying south for the winter alone and had various adventures along the way. The story's structure had something in common with *Huckleberry Finn* in that respect, they moved along and put in at ports much as Huck and Jim did with their raft. This story, though, was very much about the gander only—his mate seemed to only be along for the ride; we really never heard anything from her.

But the gander, an eye in the sky, had a real yen for adventure and an interest in the activities of the world below. So the pair would periodically swoop down in a grand spiral to join in that activity, and thus each new chapter of his story was born. This rare whimsy gave Bobby a connecting thread by which he could join all sorts of disparate episodes, but the goose remained

18 – At the Oasis

the main story, it never seemed to be an artificial device. In fact, and I suppose this was Bobby's weakness, the individual episodes themselves all seemed to need further development—they were sketchy and a bit unconvincing.

But the goose was glorious.

A Sistine Chapel of My Own

Originally published:
RE:AL The J. of Liberal Arts
Volume XXVII, Nos. 1 &2
SPRING/FALL 2002

I was almost God, that day. I was away from the world, looking down upon it, or out at it, from a different place. It looked peaceful, what I could see of it, lying there in the summer sun, but I saw it as one might see a distant galaxy through a telescope. A world was there, a complex world, perhaps a busy world, possibly even a world that could turn violent—but I was not of it. I was detached, beyond it, above it—an interested observer.

The year was 1935, and I was eleven, a boy growing up on a South Dakota farm. This epiphany had an unpretentious setting—our outhouse, which was set back into some trees about a hundred feet northwest of the house. I was sitting there in the darkened interior when I noticed a nail hole through the door in front of my face. By putting my eye up close, I could squint through the hole and see outside. The scene itself was unremarkable—the nearby trees, our house, a large white structure with a hip roof, the garden, the hog yard and the road in the distance. But I was, strangely, not a part of it. It gave me a feeling of exhilaration—of awe. I was away, in some distant place. A higher place.

I have tried to explain this experience to myself, but never with complete success. What I was looking at was something I saw every day, and something I could have seen better if I had just opened the door and stepped outside. The scene I was viewing was as ordinary as anything could be, it would seem bleak to any modern viewer, just a typical summer day on an austere South Dakota farm in the Dust Bowl era. The feeling didn't even particularly relate to the scene itself; the view in another direction would have served as well, I think.

But the nail hole was essential to the experience, as was the room, and being alone there. Being alone in that small, dark space allowed me to separate myself from the world. Perhaps no one knew I was there; perhaps no one even knew there was such a person as me; perhaps I really wasn't even a person of the ordinary world—my usual awareness of self seemed to diminish or disappear in there. I became an abstraction.

The nail hole was a tiny rift in the wall that surrounded me and separated me from the world. It allowed me to see the world outside without being part of it. I was as distant from our South Dakota farm that day as Leeuwenhoek was from the teeming life he found in a drop of water when he turned his newly invented microscope on it in 1674.

It didn't seem that way to me then, but the solitude and isolation of our life on that farm would be an alien experience for Americans today. I think that isolation played a role in my experience, and that it plays an important role in similar episodes for others. Wanderers of the desert in biblical times saw burning bushes and other fantastic things. Prisoners held in solitary confinement in the dark have been known to find a new life communing with visions there. If the environment doesn't furnish experiences that arouse the mind adequately, the mind can compensate by bringing forth its own. My nail hole experience may be denied to the modern child, beset as he or she is by a profusion of outside stimuli.

In retrospect, I think that my feeling was a feeling that often grips a connoisseur when he or she looks at a great painting or other piece of art. What is actually before the viewer is mundane, merely paint and canvas, but his mind converts it into something that transports him and causes him to lose himself in the experience. In a primitive way, I experienced the essence of art on that long ago summer day.

I tried to recapture the experience later, through that nail hole and others, with limited success. I could, and still can, get a watered-down version of the emotion that gripped me that first time, but not the whole thing.

The Thirties passed, and then the war intervened. I spent three years in Africa and Europe, and more or less forgot about the nail hole until 1947. Twelve years had gone by then, and, thanks to the GI Bill, I was in college—Iowa State College, in Ames, Iowa. In the years since, it has become Iowa State University, but it was ISC then. While I was there, I came upon an episode in a novel which described an experience very similar to the one I had as a boy.

This story was set in the Rural South. The place was a barn, rather than an outhouse, and the epiphanee was a man, rather than a boy, but his experience seemed to be identical to mine. It was a striking thing for me—the idea someone else could look out at the world through a nail hole and have that same gripping reaction. The character and the setting were fictional, but it seemed to me that the author must have had such an experience at some time. Without the reinforcement of finding this story, perhaps my own experience would eventually have been forgotten.

I lived off campus at Ames, but two close friends, Jack McElroy and Oscar Jones, had a room in the dormitory, and I spent a lot of time there. I distinctly remember sitting in that room talking with Jack about the episode in the book, and I remember that he wondered out loud about what on earth this character could find so fascinating about sitting in a darkened barn, looking out through a little hole in the wall. I don't know how we both happened to be reading the book—I was taking physics, Jack was a forestry major, Oscar was a statistician, and none of us ever took English together—but we, or at least Jack and I, were reading that story and talking about it. I would like to be more specific about that conversation, and what I told Jack about my own "nail hole" experience, but fifty years have passed, and those details are gone.

Forty-seven years after that conversation, in 1994, I was in college again, at Mankato State University, working toward an English degree in creative writing. As part of that work, I wrote a short story which was based partly on my boyhood experiences in Dakota. In it, I recounted the episode about looking out through the nail hole in the toilet door, and told about later finding the same experience described in a published novel. A few years after that, a Minnesota publisher agreed to publish a book of my short stories. We decided to call the book *Dakota Incarnate*, and the collection was to include the story with the incident about the nail hole.

As part of the process of polishing the stories into final form, I had to get down to cases about the book where the guy looked out through the hole in the barn wall. What was the name of the book, who wrote it, and what exactly did it say? My idea, back when I was writing the story, was that the passage was from *Tobacco Road*, by Erskine Caldwell, but I had not gone so far as to get a copy and confirm my recollection. Caldwell wrote many stories, but that novel, *Tobacco Road*, published in 1932, is perhaps his best-known work. It was also a hit as a Broadway play and as a movie.

Faced with the fact that my story was to appear in print, I got *Tobacco Road* from the library and paged through it, looking for the episode. I didn't find it, so I finally sat down and read the whole book. It was fun to meet Jeeter again, and Ellie May, and sobering to experience the extreme poverty and isolation of their lives, but the story came and went with no mention of anybody sitting in an old barn looking out through a tiny hole in the wall.

Well, I thought, I have apparently been remembering the wrong book. Maybe it was *God's Little Acre,* another of Caldwell's popular works. So I got that and renewed acquaintance with Darling Jill and her sisters, but met with the same lack of success as far as anybody making a big deal out of looking out through a nail hole. Wrong author, apparently, I decided. My next idea was John Steinbeck's *The Grapes of Wrath,* and soon I was back in the dust bowl of Oklahoma with the Joads, and back with the California labor problems of the 1930s. A great story, but there was nothing about what I was looking for, and I began to worry. There was a limit to how many books I could read in search of one isolated, short passage.

These books did something else for me though—they brought back the thirties. It is surprising to find how that era had such distinguishing hallmarks, and to find that its literature reflects those hallmarks in a way that a history text usually cannot. People have changed since then, in some way. It's not that they are better or worse, but they are different. Even the few who survive from that time are not the same people now.

Caldwell exaggerates; most of what he gives us in *Tobacco Road* is so extreme as to border on fantasy or burlesque, and the Rural South is far from Dakota, yet I was able to relate to his story immediately—It had a distinctive thirties "feel," and the feel resided in the way his characters thought, spoke, and acted. I doubt if the author even did this on purpose, and I doubt if a modern author could reproduce the effect, or explain it. Certainly I cannot. People were thinner, I guess, without trying to be. And even the bums and crooks had some dignity and a sort of honesty about themselves.

But time was moving on, and we needed that passage. I still knew my college friends, Jack McElroy in Texas and Oscar Jones in Atlanta, Georgia. We keep in touch by e-mail and see each other occasionally, so I wrote to Jack to ask if he remembered our conversation of fifty years earlier, and, if so, did he remember the name of the book?

"Swede," he said (using my nickname from that time), "you are out of your mind."

He did suggest that I try Oscar though, on the theory that Oscar lived in Georgia, and was of a more literary bent anyway. I did, although I don't really remember that O was even involved in the conversation about the book in the first place. At any rate, I struck out again.

Growing desperate, I began asking everyone I knew. I received many suggestions, although no one specifically remembered the passage I was looking for. Soon I was faced with the prospect of reading the combined output of two dozen prolific southern writers, and with no assurance that my passage was in the work of any of them. Some of the people obviously doubted that there ever was such a passage in the first place. They seemed to want to pat me gently on the shoulder and talk about how easy it is, after many years, to remember things that never really happened.

I contacted Kevin Langton at Mankato, a former associate familiar with southern literature. I talked with the librarian at the University of Minnesota, and she spent a whole week on it. I even wrote to the English Department at the University of Georgia, taking pains to laud them as being the focal point on Southern U.S. Literature for the entire western world. They didn't even answer.

Finally, the day came when we could wait no longer. The printer was ready to start the galley proofs. We had to go without the name of the story, or its author. I smoothed it off as best I could, and *Dakota Incarnate* was published. But the omission plagued me, and I kept looking. I became as the ancient mariner, sailing alone on an empty ship on a mission that had become meaningless.

Strangely, our vaunted modern systems of information storage and data retrieval are useless in such a quest. What we want, if it exists, is stored on a library shelf somewhere, but we really have no way of getting to it by any of the new techniques. Perhaps a day will come when mankind's literary works will all be converted into electronic data bits and stored in some gigantic, searchable data base, but it won't happen in my lifetime.

What we have – what we depend upon – is an array of millions of mass-produced human brains, each capable of storing and retrieving an astonishing amount of data, but in many formats and in idiosyncratic arrangements of limited reliability and uncertain shelf life. The retrieval system is necessarily a distributed one rather than a central one. Each person has to search through her or his own brain; we have no way of searching the brains of others.

Getting information out of this hodgepodge is an art in itself. Some obscure fact being sought may be, often is, stored in the back of someone's head somewhere, perhaps in several heads. As in a library book on a dusty shelf, unopened for decades or centuries, the fact is inside that head, as good as new, ready to spring to life when called upon.

But how to reach it? The fact sought may lie in the cobwebby recesses of only a few human brains, and may have lain there in dead storage, never consciously considered, for decades. To find it, you must make your need known to someone who has it, and convince him that he should recall it and communicate it to you. If you don't even know who he is, then you have my problem.

I wonder how much significant information has been lost forever. I suppose every person who dies takes with him or her some information that no one else knows, and that somewhere among that myriad of lost bits and bytes lies the reason they built Stonehenge, the secret that allowed Roman ballistae to throw rocks so far, old recipes for mouth-watering bread, the identity of the father of the children of Sally Hemmings, and who knows what else.

Our newspaper, *The St. Paul Pioneer Press*, includes a daily feature called "Bulletin Board." People write or call BB about all sorts of things, and the column is a compilation of their comments, with, occasionally, some brief editorial remarks. Often, one reader will open a topic, another will respond, and the discussion will continue for days. In some ways, BB resembles a print version of the chat room.

So one day I had an idea—why not send my problem in to Bulletin Board? If they would print it, it would be exposed to many of the picky, literary minds who seem to inhabit the Twin Cities area and read Bulletin Board.

So I wrote it up and sent it in. They not only printed it— they headlined it. "We're looking for a guy in an old barn," said the black print below the feature byline.

The response was less than overwhelming, but two people did write in. One told about her father, the English teacher, and suggested several southern authors. I added them to my list. The other one broke new ground. For the first time, I had reached someone, a man from Wisconsin, who thought he remembered reading such a passage.

"Try *Journeyman* by Erskine Caldwell," he suggested.

Erskine Caldwell! I rushed to our local library to check their holdings, but there was no such book there. Next, I visited the university library in Mankato. They had a modest shelf of Caldwell, but no *Journeyman*. Then, straining my computer skills to the utmost, I went into the state system, found a copy in St. Cloud, and ordered it via "ILL," which turned out to be interlibrary loan. Three weeks later, I held *Journeyman* in my trembling hands.

Eureka! I didn't even have to read it. Just paged through Caldwell's tale of the poverty stricken Rural South in the thirties, and there was the scene, a whole damn chapter, just as I remembered it from fifty years earlier. Oh, not exactly. The story had a little crack in the wall, instead of a nail hole. And there were three men, instead of just one, although two of them didn't come in until later. At first it's only the one guy, I think his name is Tom, and he's sitting on a stool with his eye glued to a tiny hole in the wall, mesmerized, just as I had seen him all along.

The other two men, one a neighboring farmer and the other an itinerant preacher, come into the yard, looking for Tom. They can't find him at first, but then a black man says, "Look in the barn, he goes there a lot." They do, and find Tom sitting on the stool, face pressed against the wall, looking out through the tiny crack. They naturally ask what in the hell he is looking at, and Tom tries to explain. His explanations sound a good deal like mine. He doesn't know, there's just something about it. There's nothing to see, other than a part of the farm no different than any other part of it or neighboring farms, and yes, he could see it better if he'd just step outside the door there, and yes, it was a scene he saw every day anyway. But there was something about looking at it this way that drew him back to this hole often.

The preacher, a domineering man, oozed scorn, but decided he'd just have a look for himself, and so Tom relinquished his place on the stool. After a few minutes of viewing, the preacher stopped to ask if there was anything in "that there jug." There was, and Tom was a convivial host, and soon the third guy was demanding a shot at the hole as well as at the jug, and they began to take turns, each yielding the stool reluctantly as the other grew impatient.

So Caldwell was familiar with the appeal of the nail hole, and apparently saw it as universal, given a proper backdrop of isolation, solitude and, perhaps, naiveté.

It's too bad that I didn't get the reference to *Journeyman* into my book, and that I didn't say more about Caldwell's story there, but I still have a feeling of joy about this whole chain of events. It shows the human mind triumphant, both subjectively and objectively.

On the objective side, I rejoice in the process that brought the two experiences, Tom's and mine, together. Imagine it—those scraps of trivia rattled around alone for decades, some in the back of my head and others in that of my benefactor from Wisconsin, and then emerged intact and joined forces to solve a problem. The human intellect builds systems, versatile systems that work. Problems find solutions.

But also, surely, to see and feel what Tom saw and felt, and what I saw and felt, is a manifestation of art at its best. Michelangelo struggled through all of his difficult life to create objects that could produce such feelings in his viewers. Yet, Tom and I and, by Caldwell's theory, everyone else, had the power to produce such subjective feelings on our own, given only a few simple props and an ordinary country scene.

There will always be great art – it comes from within.

What Can Be the Use of Them

Shadows—simple things, mechanically.
Infinitely complex in effect.
Moving, creeping—leaping, lingering,
blending, blooming—fading to darkness.
Three dimensions reduced to two.
Hyper cubes on a crap table,
snake eyes, floating like fish, everywhere.

The south side of an old barn towards evening
when the sun is nearly west.
Long, eerie, shadows—black moss on the gray wall,
springing from every irregularity,
from every protruding nail and warped board,
creeping together as the sun edges north.

Craters, huge and tiny, on the moon,
canyon walls on Mars, delineated by shadow.
The ancient precision of a sun dial.

Strange, writhing, figures on the ground
cast by children on swings and monkey bars.
A trio of horses with ten foot legs
galloping along Prairie Ridge at dawn.
Ferris wheel spokes and rocking seats
mingling through the stark limbs
and branches of a long dead cottonwood tree
on the surface of the parking lot
at the county fair.

Shifting moiré patterns from a picket fence
on a corner lot in Biwabik at sunset.

Metaphor in Poetry

"O, My love is like a red, red rose," said Robert Burns. His expression is, according to most authorities, a simile, i.e., a figure of speech in which two essentially unlike things are explicitly said to be alike. The poet could have gone further, as many do, and said, "My Love is a red, red rose." Taken in context, his readers would understand, not that he had fallen in love with a bit of plant life, but rather that the lady he loved shared some characteristic of the rose—perhaps its beauty. Taken that way, his expression would be a metaphor. Metaphor, in poetry or in prose, is a more general term than simile, and refers to figurative language generally. Such expressions as "the evening of life" are metaphor. The constructions can be more complex, but the idea is to describe something by saying or implying that it is something else—something that it, literally speaking, is not.

These two "somethings" are known as the tenor and the vehicle. "My love" would be the tenor, and "a red, red rose" would be the vehicle in the example above. With "the evening of life" it is best to first state more fully what the expression implies. The poet is speaking of some particular phase of life, and is saying that this phase bears the same relationship to life as a whole as an evening bears to its whole day. Then the particular phase of life of which he is speaking is seen to be the tenor, and the evening of the day is seen to be the vehicle.

Poetry is like music, however, in that how it sounds is of paramount importance, so poets often feel compelled to forego complete statements in favor of assonance, alliteration, rhyme, rhythm, succinctness, and a host of other artful devices. In particular, they will often omit the tenor in a metaphor and leave just the naked vehicle standing there alone. This can work well. If a poet refers to "the tears of yon cloud," most readers will be astute enough to realize that she is talking about rain, and she will be left free to manipulate her line for sensual effects. In terms of structure, her metaphor is incomplete—the tenor (the rain) is missing, but understood. In this situation, we often say that the tears of the cloud stand for rain. Sometimes we hear it said that the tears of the cloud are a metaphor for rain, but surely this is a misuse of the word.

With other incomplete metaphors, the reader may not be so sure. If a poem talks about a "red, red rose" without mentioning the "My love" part, one may get the idea that the poet is referring to courage, or to sadness, or to death, or to something else. Two different readers, after reading the same poem, may come away with two totally different ideas of what the poet is saying. Indeed, as the lines pile on one incomplete metaphor after another, a hundred readers may come away with a hundred ideas of what the poem is about, and a hundred others may confess that they have no idea what it is about, or may suspect that it is not about anything—that the poet is merely parading a string of images across the page.

A diligent reader may try to gain insight into the poet's meaning by means of external clues—the poet's life history, his other works, the political history of his time, literary references, and so forth. Some, however, find virtue in this very ambiguity, and see it as the essence of much good poetry. If a poem is capable of being read in many different ways, then each reader can read it in his or her own way, and the poem will come to be about something that is of interest to that particular reader. Certainly, if a poem is loaded with metaphors, or the naked vehicles thereof, and the reader is left to supply all or many of the tenors, then the reader can be said to have contributed a substantial part of the poem, and it does seem reasonable to suppose that the poem will then be about something that is important to the reader.

So for such a poem, a poem with a lot of images that seem to belong to incomplete metaphors, perhaps the reader should make it his or her own poem by supplying the missing tenors, and not worry about what, if anything, the poet actually had in mind. In this view, the poem is whatever we have before us on the sheet of paper – it doesn't matter where it came from, it has become a thing of its own. As Archibald McLeish put it, "A poem should not mean, but be." Such a poem is successful if it inspires its reader to pick up where the poet left off, and to go forward from there.

It seems like a risky business though, expecting the reader to furnish part of the work. For one thing, some readers may not rise to the occasion, either because they choose not to, or because they feel that they are unable to do so. And, for another, how is history to judge the poet if his poems exist complete only in the minds of his readers?

Holy Water

With apologies to James Wright and Minnesota's deformed frogs.

Over my head, I see a parking meter
perched on the black curb.
Lamplight creeps dimly along the deserted alley,
and the eyes of an exquisite green frog
greet me with kindness.
She has come gladly from her iridescent puddle
to welcome my bottle and me.
I roll nearer. She has three legs and black spots
glisten upon her back. She is alone
and I am new to the gutter – a fugitive
from suburbia. Her throat ripples tensely.
I smile and wave my fingers.
She likes me! It has been lonely for her here.
She bows enchantingly, shy as a wet swan. I am
undone.
Later I doze and dream. A sex partner
with three legs. Delicious warm wetness. Ecstasy.

When I wake she is beside me,
throat full-voluptuous, eyes skyward
charting Orion's course, serenading his passage.
I would like to hold her slender body
for she has hopped over to me
and pressed against my hand on the pavement.

She is lithe, solemn, serene.
Her tongue flashes and is gone, a rapier
Impales a fly in mid-air.
A light breeze moves me to caress her silken back,
delicate as the bark of a May willow shoot.

Suddenly I weep for those lost years of sobriety.
I have wasted my life.

Holy Water was originally published in *Poet Lore* (Vol. 96, No. 3, Fall/Winter, 2001.

Old Soldiers

"Mornin' Sam," I said, sliding onto the stool closest to the coffee pot, and curling my legs around the post under it.

"Mornin' Bill," he answered.

Renee was hurrying by with two plates of eggs and hash browns, but she shot a glance my way and I nodded. Seconds later my coffee was in front of me and I knew that an order of wheat toast would not be far behind.

"Did you see this morning's paper?" asked Sam. "That goddam Bush is shooting off his mouth again. I think he's got war on the brain."

"Yeah. I don't know what's the matter with them down there. It seems as if they've got no common sense of any kind."

Sam is, like me, a veteran of WWII. We have been praised as the greatest generation, but most of us now, in a peculiar way, feel left out of today's world. Other people write about us all of the time, and often in laudatory terms, but their tendency is to reduce the WWII vet to a cliché, and the war itself to a myth—to something akin to the American West. No one hears from us directly, so we feel somewhat alone and misunderstood, and talk to each other. And the war is so long ago now that even we aren't always sure if we're remembering it, or just remembering what we've heard about it. So mostly we don't actually talk about the war. We talk about the army, or about the places we visited, or about current events in light of our wartime experiences.

When the war ended, Sam's unit was sent to Japan, so he was there for about six months before he got to come home. He likes to talk about Japan—says they have good beer over there. This has led him into a certain amount of conflict with Gerhardt Roettger, who often occupies another stool at the Oasis. Gerhardt, fifty plus years after leaving Japan, still complains about the beer he was served there.

"It seems to me that Roosevelt and the people that were running the show back then had a lot better judgment and more common sense," I said. "You were in Japan after the war. Didn't that go pretty smooth?"

"Well, I don't know," he said. "It seemed to, but then I was just a sort of a private in the rear rank. MacArthur was the big shot. What the hell would I know?"

"Did you like Japan?" I asked him.

"Well, of course I'd been gone a long time and was anxious to get home. I had enough points, so I bitched because I thought it wasn't fair for them to keep me there that long, but actually it was pretty good duty."

"I suppose," I said with a wink at Kim, "but I was talking with Gerhardt Roettger about it one day here, and he told me that the beer in Japan is really bad."

Sam snorted. "That goddam Roettger is full of shit. The reason he says that is because he didn't come to Japan until after I'd left. By then the Americans had drunk up all of the good beer, and it took a long time for them to get organized to make more. I heard that the stuff they put out for a while there wasn't much better than swill. But that wasn't the real Japanese beer. Roettger doesn't know what he's talking about."

"Well," I conceded, "I think he is a year or two younger than us, so he maybe didn't get into the army until after the war."

"Yeah, but that ain't my point," answered Sam. "I don't hold that against him. He can't help when he was born. All I say is that the Japs make a damn good beer."

We were silent for a while, until finally I asked, "Did you ever think about going back to Japan for a visit, Sam?"

I expected him to snort again, but he didn't. Instead, he grew thoughtful, and a far away look took possession of his eye. "I don't know," he said. "It's too late now—I'm too goddam old. I used to think about it once in a while. I wonder what it would have been like."

Ansbach Again

It had been 42 years, but I somehow didn't expect the town to be much changed. My ticket from Geneva indicated that the train would arrive in Ansbach, a small city in Bavaria, at 6:47 that evening. As trains in Europe are wont to do, this one screeched to a halt beside the platform in Ansbach at 6:47 pm.

I had been stationed here in 1952, during the Korean War, as a lieutenant in the 979th Field Artillery Battalion. We periodically spent a week or two with our guns in position along the Iron Curtain, supposedly to hold off the Russians. Otherwise we lived a garrison life in Ansbach, and frolicked at the DrechselsGarten and the Grauer Wolf, two local bistros.

But this was 1994. I had taken my two grandsons to Geneva to visit my son, Brad, and his family. He is an economist there. During our stay, I decided to leave the boys with Brad for a few days and pay a nostalgic visit to Ansbach.

I wandered through the bahnhof with my bag, but the station appeared to be new or rebuilt, so I went out onto the street and tried to get my bearings. That failed too, so I began to walk through the streets, which seemed to be generally familiar, but saw nothing specific that I recognized. Ansbach is old and has 38,000 inhabitants, but it is compact and looks smaller. Although there are many cars, the automobile is not king as it is in America. The town is built in a hilly area, so the streets snake around in a haphazard manner. there are many, especially downtown, that are narrow and winding and meet in a hodge-podge of distinctive intersections. Most of the buildings along such streets are made of stone, and crowd close to narrow sidewalks. Sometimes there is no sidewalk at all, and one steps from the building directly into the traveled portion of the street.

Darkness was approaching, and I needed a place to stay, so when I came upon a door with a sign that said "Hotel und Gasthof

36 – At the Oasis

Birnbaum, Nurnberger Strasse," I rang the bell. A motherly frau stuck her head out of an upstairs window and quizzed me, then came down and let me in. It turned out to be a very nice place with a well-furnished room and bath. German style bedding, but nice—looked new. In my experience, most German beds use what we call a duvet, rather than sheets and blankets.

A duvet, properly speaking, is a comforter or tick stuffed with feathers, or down, and enclosed in a sack like a giant pillowcase. The sack is intended to be removed for laundering. One can buy a duvet, usually a very fancy one, in an American department store, but most people do not. Duvet comes from the French word for down, such as eiderdown or swansdown, but the French refer to this item as a couette. To the Germans, it is das federbett, while the British say duvet, or, rather sniffily, continental quilt. In the wartime federbetts that I was used to, the sack tended to be made of coarse, scratchy, muslin, and the innards partly of straw, or at least something other than the soft breast under plumage of eider ducks or swans. The biggest trouble with them was that they were not very flexible—you could not, by any means, wrap yourself up in those duvets. Instead, they perched on top of you, and left an open channel along each side of your body through which cold air could circulate freely.

But the federbett at the Birnbaum was warm, flexible, and the cover was made of a crisp and soft, finely woven, white, percale that smelled of sunshine and fresh air. In fact, the whole place seemed to have been recently remodeled. The price was 75 Deutsch Marks ($50) per night, including breakfast. I was pleased. I had heard lots of tales about people paying $200 a night for hotel rooms all over Europe.

It so happened that there was a big celebration going on in Ansbach that week—The Ansbacher Kirchweih und Schutenfest. I didn't know what that meant, but the flyer said it was a Grosser Vergnugungspark, and located near the hotel, so I went to have a look. It turned out to be a carnival with bumper cars, rides, food booths, and games of skill, but the main deal was the beer garden. It included the biggest tent I ever saw—looked to be about the size of a football field. Inside, it was filled with people seated on benches at sturdy wooden tables, plus a 12 piece German brass band on a center stage. A big sign on the end wall said it was the Festhall.

A waiter sold me a mug of beer that must have held close to half-a-gallon (1.5 liter?) and I sat down to watch and listen. The band struck up "The Laughing Polka" and about half the people got up on top of their tables waving their beer mugs and started to dance. They were definitely having a good time. The band mixed the music up—some polkas, but also a lot of what seemed to be polka rock. It was wild. I thought once that I saw my friend, Frank Elles, standing on one of the benches in his characteristic hunched over stance.

Frank and I had a lot in common—we had come into the army from the Michigan National Guard together, had trained together at Fort McCoy in Wisconsin, and held equivalent jobs in different batteries while we were in Germany. Frank also had a little MG sports car, and I went places with him often. I especially remember a trip we took to Munich, where we visited the famous Hofbrau Haus, and then went on to Salzburg and Vienna. I have a snapshot of Frank that I took while we were aboard a troopship, returning home from Germany, and it is by that image that I remember him best. We were in the English Channel, and he is standing beneath some lifeboat davits, looking out toward the White Cliffs of Dover, which can be dimly seen in the distance.

Now, it seemed, I was seeing him again—grinning and waving his mug at the band while yelling the name of some song he wanted them to play. I almost tried to make my way over to him, but I realized that he couldn't possibly still look like that after 42 years, so it had to be someone else. Even so, I suddenly felt a little bit at home, and the thought came to me that I should keep some notes about my Ansbach visit, and then write up an account of it and send it to several friends from those days, including Frank, Tom Flanagan and Ray Nelson.

It was near midnight in Ansbach by then. I hadn't had dinner, so I went to a food booth where they had some huge pork hocks that looked like hams, and tried to order something to eat. The guy asked me something (halbe?) which I didn't understand at the time, so I shook my head and pointed at the pork hocks. He shook his head (crazy American) and gave me a whole one. It was huge, and he charged me about $14, but it was very good and I was hungry, so I drank another beer and ate most of it.

38 - At the Oasis

In 1952 we had been stationed at a kaserne here. These are common in many German towns as places to quarter troops. Ansbach had three—ours was the Bleidorn Kaserne. It consisted of about five acres of cobblestone-covered land surrounded by a high fence or wall. Inside the wall were large barracks adequate for about 1000-2000 men, plus offices, classrooms, mess halls, garages, maintenance shops, and warehouses. Outside the wall, on one side of the kaserne, was a cluster of apartment houses for "dependent housing," home to the families of those soldiers who had wives and children there. All told, Bleidorn, which overlooked Ansbach from a hilltop on the edge of town, was a small American colony on German soil.

In 1994, when I walked out to Bleidorn and looked through the locked main gate, I found it closed and deserted with grass and weeds growing up through the cobblestones. I was reminded of the old Dakota country school I attended for eight years so long ago, and of my grandma's farm nearby—once so busy and vital, now deserted and standing in ruins like so many Midwest farms, schools, and country churches. As these scenes often do, Bleidorn gave me an eerie feeling of a dropped stitch in the fabric of time— Twilight Zone come to life.

The dependent housing apartments outside Bleidorn were still in use by Americans, most of them were stationed at Katterbach, another town further east on the road toward Nuremberg. Bleidorn was closed in 1992, but part of it had been reopened later to house refugees from Bosnia. Looking at it there, one had to wonder if the real purpose was to house these refugees or to jail them. Inside the wall, a very, very high new fence had been built around the two barracks buildings that had housed A and B Batteries in our day, and there was a new gate into that part. Some German people at the beer garden (I went back) told me that there was talk that the Ansbach Police Department might take over Bleidorn.

One of the other kasernes had been abandoned and razed to make way for new construction, but the third one was still occupied by American troops, so I went there to look around. As a military installation it differed but little from what those places had been in the fifties—a little more relaxed and less formal, perhaps. The kaserne itself looked OK, though a little scruffy—like an old shoe. It seemed to symbolize a marked change that I noticed everywhere. The American presence in town was much diminished from what we had known. Partly, this was because there were fewer troops, and even those few either kept to themselves or wore civilian clothes and blended in. Gone were the days when raucous Americans in uniform crowded the bars and streets. Gone were the days when I led convoys of tanks and trucks through these narrow streets on almost a daily basis. One could now almost live in Ansbach for weeks at a time without even being aware that there was an American army around—a good thing, I thought. A sign that the world was returning to normal.

But, to an even greater extent, the diminished American presence was the result of the changes in the town itself. In 1952, Ansbach still had a gray, somber look, little changed from its wartime persona. Streetlights were few and dim, and traffic was light. There were few people about on the streets, and they often seemed to eye each other warily. Signs were subdued, as were the clothes that people wore, and paint was scarce. War does that. I had been in Germany, although not in Ansbach, during the war (WWII), and so this look was familiar to me. Many cities, and large parts of others, had been reduced to rubble, and the parts not rubble were characteristically dark and sparsely peopled. Ansbach was essentially untouched by the fighting—there had been only one air raid, apparently aimed at the railroad yards. To the great amusement of the Germans, most of the bombs had missed the town completely. We had bombed the very shit out of a forest west of town though, they said. Actually, their mastery of American idiom wasn't good enough for them to put it exactly that way. "Many bombs fall in woods," would be more of a literal quote.

But now, in 1994, there is none of this—no darkness, no furtive shadows scuttling across a few open spaces. Instead, the town shines. Traffic is heavy, and people in colorful clothes throng the sidewalks. Bright lights illuminate the reconstructed streets, and everyone is comfortable and busy there. America is the furthest thing from their minds.

On my way there I had imagined that I would meet some old friends—Germans that I had known. I didn't remember their names, of course, or at least not their last names, but I imagined that I would run into them on the streets, or in the Gasthaus or the bar. After a few hours in the new Ansbach it was apparent that such an idea was ridiculous. Such people would be old now, possibly dead, or moved away. Even if I saw some of them among these throngs, I probably wouldn't recognize them. And people my age don't hang out in the busy bars of today.

And even if I did, against all odds, meet some of them, they probably wouldn't remember me anyway. An experience like Ansbach is unique for someone like me, but for a German in the town I would represent only a brief interlude in a succession of American soldiers who came and went. In their eyes, we must be generic. So nostalgia is probably more appropriate to places than to people there. The best I could do was to recall the people while looking at the places.

With this in mind, I went to check out the Gray Wolf, a bistro, dance hall, and restaurant combo where we had enjoyed many good times. I had to ask directions to get myself oriented, but then went through the gate by the castle and the street was just as it had always been. The place still looked the same on the outside, a kind of an A-frame structure in white stucco with exposed beams. The same Grauer Wolf sign was still there, and the metal wolf still hung from the arm that sticks out into the street from the second floor, so I felt a surge of pleasure as one does when coming home after a long absence. I had been warned, however, that the place had been converted to a disco joint, so I didn't go in. Why spoil the memory?

On the way back I noticed two memorials on the church wall a little way down the street—one to the German dead from WWI and one for WWII. These were bronze plates engraved with the names of the men and boys from Ansbach who had been killed in those conflicts. I didn't remember these plaques, but they must have been there when we were. I was immediately reminded of a similar plaque in the country church near Nunda, South Dakota, that we attended when I was a child, and of similar plaques in so many places in America. The one in our church was for WWI and contained thirteen names arranged in two rows of six, with Sylvester Schnell's name centered at the bottom. Most of the thirteen were men I knew, men who, as youths, had gone off to war six or seven years before I was born, and had returned to live out their lives in our farming community.

The number of names on the plaques in Ansbach was much greater than thirteen, and the names were those of men and boys who had never returned. In spite of this monumental difference, there was a sameness about the plaques that caused me to reflect again upon the huge cultural history and the many mores that we share with our enemy in any war.

I also visited DrechselsGarten, another favorite watering hole on the top of another hill on another edge of town. Big surprise—it's still there, but the place we knew has been replaced by a very fancy hotel, restaurant, and nightclub. A room there would probably have easily hit that $200 mark. I had a beer in the hotel bar during happy hour and wanted some sort of a souvenir, so I tried to explain to the girl bartender who I was and why I was there, but she didn't understand or didn't care, or both. Luckily, though, there were two hard-charging, local, young German businessmen at the bar who spoke English well, and they took quite an interest in my story. "You're an American? And you were stationed here in Ansbach forty-two years ago?" one asked in disbelief. "Yeah," I said, "we used to come here quite often, but the place looks entirely different now." He explained about the new hotel and where the old place had been. I told him I had failed to get some sort of a keepsake of the place from the bartender. "Oh, to hell with her," he said, and reached across the bar to grab a little coaster with the DrechselsGarten name on it. "Here, stick this in your pocket."

Ansbach also has a castle. I had never been inside while we were stationed there, so I signed up for a tour. It was amazing. They don't call it a castle but a "Residence." It was once an old-time castle with battlements, a moat, and a drawbridge, but was rebuilt after the castle era and became the home of the "Margrave." It consists of a huge, box-like structure with three main stories, if memory serves me right. Each story has a wide hall around the periphery, and rooms of many kinds in the interior—ballrooms, bedrooms, dining rooms, drawing rooms—it goes on and on, and each room is loaded with priceless works of art.

After Napoleon won a war there, Ansbach was ceded to Bavaria. The Bavarian government took over the castle then, and has preserved it ever since. It remains essentially as it was in 1805, with its paintings, tapestries, porcelain, and furniture. The Margrave's wife was a sister to Frederick the Great of Prussia, so many of these artifacts were gifts from him. Some of the paintings are by famous artists—Vandyke, for example. The place is, in fact, a museum as well as a historic site. I can't imagine what it must be worth—certainly many, many millions.

After I got home, I wrote up an account of my visit to send to others who had been stationed at Ansbach with me—three men in particular who had been close friends. I had addresses for two of them, but not for Frank Elles from Michigan, the guy who I briefly imagined seeing that first night at the Festhall. The Internet White Pages showed a phone under that name, so I tried to call—and tried and tried, but no one ever answered. Finally, I sent a letter to the address listed, which was only a town and a zip, but it came back for insufficient address. This went on for two years as I found progressively better clues, until I finally got an address that appeared to be his wife, Suzie, in a different city. I had known her too, so I wrote, and finally did get a response, although not a happy one. Frank had died in 1990, and they had separated some time before that. The phone number I had tried to call for so long was a cabin he had owned at Irons, MI. Why the phone still rang, I'll never know. More Twilight Zone, I guess.

I was shocked to hear of Frank's death, and saddened by the loss of the opportunity to visit with him about our old days in Ansbach, and by whatever had occurred to cause him and Suzie to go their separate ways so long ago. But one thing was good—she obviously remembered him fondly, as I remember both of them. Suzie sent me a memorial card that features a pen-and-ink sketch of Frank done by their daughter, who is clearly talented. The sketch shows Frank (head and shoulders) aboard another ship in New York Harbor, with the Statue of Liberty in the background. He is bearded, wearing glasses and a baseball cap with scrambled eggs on the visor. The years have treated him well—he looks harder, less ready to laugh, perhaps, but still very much Frank Elles.

Writing this now makes me want to go back to Ansbach again. It's a strange idea, I suppose, since I speak German hardly at all, and don't know a soul there. But who can account for what appeals to us. Perhaps I'll go to celebrate turning eighty, an event that is looming near. I'll stay at the DrechselsGarten, in one of those two hundred dollar rooms, and then I'll go down to the bar, order a beer, and drink a toast to that black girl, who was such a steady customer at the old DrechselsGarten and who, in fits of exuberance, would often get up and dance on top of the bar.

Guatemala Journey

Our last sight of San Miguel Conacaste was the tractor—sitting, as always, on the edge of the town square with its plow and disc harrow nearby. I was never able to find anybody who would tell me about the tractor. It was a heavy duty model 185 Massey-Ferguson, 1950s vintage, and potentially able to do a lot of work, but I was sure it would never run again. Among other things, the three point lift was torn apart and open to the weather and the big tires were in very bad shape. It must have been a major investment for the Conacaste Farmers Cooperative (COOP) and they hadn't been in business all that long.

Manuel's father told me that a man comes from Sanarate with a tractor and plow; they paid him thirty quetzals per manzana. That would be about $17/acre, a big price even at home. I'm sure that paying to have the fields plowed represents a major expense, and I imagine that their tractor was to be a savior. I don't think there are any tractor mechanics in Conacaste, either to maintain the machine or to judge its condition before purchase; I'm afraid that the COOP was taken for a ride, a ride that they could ill afford. At any rate, the tractor sat there, and probably sits there still, a brooding monument to a misguided effort undertaken with good intentions and poor judgment.

The guy that got me into this was Jimmy Carter. I turned on the TV one day and there he was in overalls and hard hat, crawling across a room in a Bronx tenement, resolutely slamming nails into a new floor with his twenty ounce claw hammer. It was enough to stir the most jaded do-gooder to action, and I felt sure that I knew more about pounding nails than he did. He was working for "Habitat for Humanity," an organization dedicated to solving the social ills of America by using volunteer labor to construct affordable housing for poor people.

44 – At the Oasis

We were "Global Volunteers". (GV) is a sort of a short-term, pay-your-own-way, privately operated Peace Corps. They send "teams" to various undeveloped foreign countries to help the locals with some community project there. Great stress is laid upon this; the project must originate with the locals. GV has headquarters in St. Paul and works in a number of countries including India, Poland, Mexico, Paraguay, Guatemala, Tanzania and others. I signed on with a team that was headed for Guatemala in February 1991, for sixteen days. The cost was $1650, including airfare.

Our team was very small—four volunteers plus a team leader hired by GV. We met at the airport gate in Dallas (wearing our GV t-shirts so we could find each other), and then boarded a flight for Guatemala City, where we would meet the team leader, Ray.

Our ultimate destination, Sam Miguel Conacaste, lay, we had been told, about fifty miles east of Guatemala City along the main road toward Belize. It is in a Spanish speaking area; some parts of Guatemala speak neither Spanish nor English, but retain, instead, a language based on the original Indian dialect. Our sponsoring organization, the International Cultural Institute (ICI) was making a determined effort to help villages like Conacaste develop tools to cope with their economic and cultural situation. Conacaste was a center of sorts for this effort—some things had been developed as a model for other villages to emulate, and people from other villages came there to attend meetings where the ICI demonstrated and discussed innovations in agriculture, health, and municipal services. A center had been constructed—concrete block with corrugated steel roof. Part of it is two stories, a dormitory of sorts where we would stay. There was also a kitchen and an open area with a sunshade roof, plus another single story row of small rooms, and an area with three toilets and a sink. It was plush, as these things go there, perhaps the only place in Latin America where Global Volunteers had the use of sit-down flush toilets, even though the flushing was done with a bucket of water from a barrel and used toilet paper had to be put into a box, (never, under any circumstances, into the toilet), and the toilets had no seats.

I was 67 at the time, a retired industrial physicist. Bryan was a businessman from Dubuque, Iowa, whose brother had been killed in Viet Nam. He was 42, married, with children, and of Greek ancestry—he had visited relatives in rural Greece. Politically, he was liberal, very concerned about many social problems, including those of Latin America. Margit, 32, was a schoolteacher from Boise, Idaho. She had taught elementary school in southern Texas, so she had experience with Spanish speaking children. Margit's husband had been killed on a mountain climbing trip in China several years earlier (actually, more accurately, had died from altitude sickness). She had since recovered from the loss, and was seeing another guy. An independent girl, she turned out to also be a reasonable and very caring person. Stephen was also in his early forties, from Seattle, single, an environmental engineer who worked with city water systems.

At the airport in Guatemala City it took a while to get all of our junk together since we were equipped as for a camping trip. We made our way through customs, which was organized in an efficient, if somewhat primitive manner, and finally emerged onto the sidewalk to meet Ray, and the GV pickup truck. Ray was about 45, originally from Minnesota, but had mostly moved to Central America—he had bought some land to develop in Costa Rica. He is something of a character from a Mitchner novel, tall and thin with red hair and beard. Manuel and Alfredo were with Ray, they work for the ICI. Both were very familiar with San Conacaste. It was, in fact, Manuel's original home and his parents still lived and farmed there.

It was about 10 at night, and warm. The air reminded me of the warm summer nights that often followed hot July days in my native South Dakota. Dropping into that from February in Minnesota gave me, and perhaps all of us, a feeling of exhilaration. We threw our stuff into the back of the truck, climbed in after it, and headed through Guatemala City scenes and traffic for the hotel, checked in, and adjourned to a local pub to have a beer and get acquainted. To Ray's obvious discomfort, and in spite of his efforts to head the conversation elsewhere, the gringos in the group kept bringing it back to politics. He finally pointed out firmly that discussing politics with Guatemalans can endanger their lives. As Margit wrote in our journal, "There was a short, stunned silence. After that, we stayed off the subject."

46 – At the Oasis

The next day, Saturday, we had a meeting and looked around town for a while. Our hotel was near the government center and plaza, so it was interesting to look around there. The building reminded me of an old courthouse, except that it was large, and some of the second floor rooms had been given over to troop billets.

Shortly before noon we loaded into the pickup and headed for our village, about three hours away. We tried to get Margit to ride in front, but she was adamant, so Steve rode shotgun, Ray drove, Bryan, Margit and I crawled into the open cargo box on top of the luggage, and off we went along the main road toward Belize. It was said to be the most modern road in Guatemala, and has cut the travel time to the east coast to a fraction of what it once was, but I-35 it was not. The road travels through fairly rough country with many turns and steep grades, and is clogged with traffic, all moving at the highest possible speed and passing indiscriminately on hills and curves. It is not quite as bad as it looks. The curves have widened shoulders that provide certain flexibility, and the drivers have an engaging live-and-let-live bonhomie. Even so, it was apparent on this, and several later rides, that the danger in what we were doing by riding in the back of that truck dwarfed any peril we might conceivably face from Guatemalan gunmen.

Finally we turned off the highway onto a narrow lane, which we followed for several miles through farms and fields to San Miguel Conacaste. This tiny place, in various stages of disrepair, extends only a few blocks in any direction and houses a few hundred citizens. It has grown there since the demise of the huge sugar plantations that dominated this area before they were broken up, and an old town pump still marks what was the only road intersection here in those days. To a large extent, places like Conacaste have been created by the population explosion; the denuded state of the once green surrounding hills can be traced to the same cause.

Once there, we were introduced to Patronna (50?) and Jesusa(30?). Patronna was to be our cook. She was from Conacaste, and lived with her family a short distance away. She was not only an excellent cook but also a very personable lady, a take-charge type, and a village leader. She did not speak English. Jesusa was from Peru, and did speak English. She worked for the ICI, and was there as our contact with the host organization. She was a quiet person and, unfortunately, did not feel well most of the time that we were there—proving, I suppose, that Montezuma's revenge does not fall upon the gringo alone.

The streets (trails?, alleys?) were often crowded with pigs, chickens and kids; and a smudge of smoke hung over the town most of the time. The people were friendly and happy with us and with each other to an extent that was almost inspirational. The smoke came from cooking fires and burning garbage. To the north there was a high hill that overlooked the town. A large, weather beaten, wooden Cross stood at the top of the hill, so we walked up there that evening at sunset. To the west, seventy miles away, we could see the three volcanic peaks around Antigua. One of them was smoking as we watched it. When darkness began creeping in we returned to the village. It was, after all, Saturday night, so we decided to check out the nightlife. There were three bars; each consisted of one tiny room. There were only a few people, but they were friendly and the beer was good, so we enjoyed ourselves.

Night came, but San Conacaste never sleeps. Dogs carry the main chorus until the roosters start to drown them out about 3am, but the turkeys are always there in the background and an occasional really loud pig breaks it up nicely. At least one radio, at max volume, seems to keep the whole town in touch with the outside world throughout the night, although it only becomes noticeable after the gospel singers shut down about an hour before midnight. They surprised us all. The Evangelical churches have made great inroads against the traditional Roman Catholic faith in Latin America. The new President of Guatemala was, we found, himself an Evangelical minister. Even San Conacaste has a meeting hall. It was a couple of blocks from us and very active; their hymns rolled across the rooftops on most evenings.

Our main project in Conacaste involved a community center building already under construction. It was needed to accommodate meetings of people from other villages who came there to learn about the COOP, the irrigation project, and other innovations. It would also be used for community purposes—weddings, dances, fiestas, whatever. It was to be a single story concrete block building, about 30 X 65 feet, and had progressed to the point that the walls were partly up.

48 – At the Oasis

The foreman, Israel, was the only person being paid; we were to work with him and with the village volunteers. They changed daily and ranged from young to old—from little kids and guys home on military leave up to Oscar Morales Vasquez, who was about my age. The stuff they had to work with was incredibly bad—a few boards that had to double as scaffolding and concrete pouring forms, a wheelbarrow, two shovels, a hoe, some buckets, a few trowels and a chalk line. The blocks were equally bad; they were weak and crumbly, seemed to have very little cement in them. With such blocks one cannot make a serviceable block wall as we would know it, so a different method (Post and Beam) construction is used. It depends on concrete posts and beams made with rebar; the blocks really only fill in the spaces, although they also support the beams while they are being poured. Scaffolding is made by piling up blocks into rickety stacks, and laying the form boards on top. It's lucky that no one was hurt.

Margit was pleased when we started working there. Women don't wear pants in Conacaste, so Margit had been cautioned to wear a skirt all of the time. She was indignant about this, but had a special dispensation to wear slacks while engaged in working on the building. I guess women don't lay concrete blocks there either, so it was a special situation that would tolerate a special rule.

That first day of working on the Community Center, and the abysmal inefficiency of what we were doing, brought me back to some misgivings that had occurred to me about Global Volunteers when I signed on. Was this an organization dedicated to improving the lot of people in undeveloped countries? Or was it a travel agency with a gimmick—a travel agency selling tax-deductible vacations? Including incidental expenses, the trip was going to cost me about $2000. What if I just sent the money to Guatemala instead, how would that compare? With my $2000, I felt sure, they could hire the best block layer in Guatemala for several months. On the other hand, who could think of this as a vacation? Would anyone be so foolish as to go to a native village, sleep with the pigs, work like a dog, expose himself to danger, and call it a vacation? Well, perhaps some would. In fact, now that it is over, I do look back upon it that way.

The GV spin on this was to announce, up front, that we would probably accomplish little or nothing in a physical sense.

But this was unimportant, they said. The important thing would be that the people would see us there trying to help, and we would see them and come to understand their problems. World fellowship would be promoted, etc. I was not willing to reconcile myself to the idea that we weren't going to get anything done, but I did have to admit that the venture could never be cost effective. Actually, I guess I was asking the wrong question anyway. One should really examine something like this from the point of view of our government—were the taxpayers getting anything of value in return for subsidizing this trip? But that seemed to be too complicated a question for me, so I went back to doing the best that I could at laying blocks and weeding cabbage.

On Monday, our first day of work, we worked on the Community Center from 7 -11 am, had a cervesa (beer) at the Tienda (tiny store), and then sat down to Patronna's excellent lunch of tortillas, black beans, guacamole, broccoli and coffee—and ate too much. After that we took a short siesta, and then visited and worked on farms for two or three hours. This was to be our daily routine. The Tienda was run by Anna, she apparently had the only refrigerator in the town because people often came in to buy a tablespoon of butter.

But before that, on Sunday, we had a tour around the Conacaste countryside and some of its farms. The tour was conducted by Chico, who was the head of the COOP (Farmers Cooperative), and a farmer himself. Chico spoke English quite well. It turned out that he had lived in New York for several years, and that his family was still in the U.S. Surprisingly, we met several others in Conacaste who had lived in the U.S. for brief periods.

The mainstay of the valley farmers was an irrigation system that they had built with their own labor and help from a U.N. agency. Two 125 horsepower pumps at the river pumped water about two miles over high hills to a large concrete tank on a hill above the valley. From there it ran by gravity, through pipes, to the individual farms where it was distributed down the rows by perforated plastic tubing. The system was manufactured in Israel; it also provided a way for the farmer to distribute fertilizers, insecticides and herbicides by adding them to the water.

50 – At the Oasis

The other major innovation was a potable water system. It featured a well in the valley floor that pumped water to a storage tank on the hill by the Cross. The water was distributed from there by underground pipes to the houses in the village. I'm not sure how potable the water really was; the tank was not sealed. Water was usually only available for a few hours in the morning each day—they all filled their barrels at that time. This was, no doubt, part of the reason there was no water later.

The crops were what we would call truck garden: tomatoes, cucumbers, broccoli, corn. They were raising several crops each year now, instead of one, because of the irrigation. They also had a big problem with a blight that was demolishing their major crop, tomatoes. Whether or not this was connected with the change to more intensive agriculture was a question that was on everyone's lips. On his own farm, Chico had tried to supplement the irrigation system with two hand-dug wells. One gave lots of water, the other, none. The digging of them must have been a huge job. All of the farmers were using lots of herbicides, insecticides, and high nitrogen fertilizer from Sweden. How much information did they have about all of this stuff? Nobody seemed to be able to answer, so I don't know. When I got home I tried to find out if any technical help was available for them. That inquiry went nowhere except that I did get chewed out by a Florida farmer who claimed that he was being driven to the wall by unfair competition from Latin America.

One afternoon we went to a house where they made little baskets for sale at the market in Guatemala City. They had a production line of family members sitting outdoors in the shade— a true cottage industry of seven years standing. We were again struck by the dignity and friendliness of these people for each other, a family of neighbors was there visiting with them when we came. When the neighbors left, they shook hands all around— shook arms would be a better term, they grasp each other above the elbow instead of by the hand. Margit said that this custom is unique to Guatemala. Living conditions in the village have to be seen to be understood, but I came to realize that there were important social values in San Conacaste too. Values that are not always present in our own lives—in many ways I was again reminded of life in rural South Dakota back in the thirties.

Our farm work consisted of such things as picking coffee beans, shelling corn and weeding tomatoes—plus a lot of talking and tours of the houses, kitchens, barns and fields. One of the places we visited was Patronna's house; another was the home of Manuel's parents, who were gracious hosts. They and their place especially reminded me of South Dakota farms and farmers in the thirties, even though it is physically quite different from that. The house had a long, low shaded patio across the west side. It was apparent that much of their time was spent there; the area was cluttered with chairs, tools, corn, buckets, and many other items. The kitchen was of special interest, and Manuel's mother conducted a tour of it with obvious pride. Steve was not impressed; their stoves have no proper chimney, only a hole in the roof above the spot on the stove where the smoke and fumes come out, so some of the combustion products end up in the room rather than outside. He was sure that continued exposure to this was very unhealthy for them. The stove top is large; the fire is routed around under it to heat certain areas, including an area used for making tortillas. She made one for us, after dexterously spinning the dough around in her hands to form it, and then offered us a chance to make one. Bryan and Margit each had a go at it, but with indifferent results. Only Margit's effort made it as far as the stove, "an ugly small thing," she described it—but it tasted okay.

Saturday, after a full week there, we left the village to go to Antigua, a tourist type town, to stay overnight. In Antigua we rubbed elbows with rich tourists from all over the world, listened to marimba bands in the hotel court, and enjoyed the spectacular scenery. Antigua is subject to frequent earthquakes and volcanic eruptions. It was the capital of Guatemala for many years until they finally got tired of rebuilding it. Shortly after we got home a story broke about an American nun who had been abducted, tortured and raped there, apparently by the police. She had been teaching elementary school, and had been warned to stop saying some of the thing that she was telling her pupils.

On the way there, in Guatemala City, we were met by Charles Winkler, the Guatemala head of Foster Parents, Inc. (now PLAN INTERNATIONAL). I had contacted him because I had sponsored a boy (Luis Roberto) in Guatemala for many years and wondered if it would be possible to meet him. Luis Roberto was fifteen. I had been getting letters from him for about ten years, so I had a pictorial record of him and his sisters and their mother that ran all through his childhood. Luis lived in Guatemala City, and my request worked out famously. Winkler turned out to be a prototype diplomat; it was hard to escape the conclusion that he must have been trained by the State Department. He visited with us for a half hour or so about Latin America, Guatemala, Global Volunteers and PLAN; then furnished me with a car and driver, a social worker and an interpreter. Obviously, they don't often get a visit from a sponsoring parent. Bryan came with me while the others went on to Antigua in the GV pickup. Bryan and I went out to Luis Roberto's house like a couple of visiting VIPs. The only things lacking to make us ambassadors were flags on the fenders and a siren.

Luis lived in a former slum area where PLAN had been working on community development for a number of years, and was now preparing to move on. The work that had been done was very apparent, rows of houses and sidewalks, all neat and clean— all on a miniature scale. The houses were probably not larger than 12 by 15 feet, and there were no streets between them, only sidewalks and small yards. The people along the way were well dressed and friendly. It seemed as if it wouldn't be a bad place to live.

Luis, obviously primed for the visit, was waiting on the sidewalk as we approached his area. It was great to meet him after all of those years of pictures and letters. He proved to be a well-mannered, quiet boy; tall, but of slight build. He liked school, especially math, he said, and wanted to go to the University of Guatemala and become an engineer—good news. The bad news was that he lived in the worst house in the neighborhood, cardboard box walls, corrugated steel roof, a clean pig sty—no adults around, only Luis and his younger sister. Still worse news was that PLAN was discontinuing work in that neighborhood and would be dropping him.

He graciously invited us into his house, which you could only enter by stooping down to get under the projecting corrugated steel sheets that formed a roof. In the semi-dark inside we found a bed, a table, some chairs and a television set. His sister, about twelve, bustled up, friendly and shy, and we all had quite a visit (mostly through the interpreter, of course). Luis had a pet yellow bird that they both were fond of. Bryan had a camera, so we had photo-ops too and I still cherish those pictures.

The family situation was murky. Luis answered my question about his mother and his little sister by saying that they didn't live there anymore, or at least I thought that was his answer. The social worker said afterwards that I had misunderstood, that she was at work, but I didn't think so, and the interpreter agreed with me. I had just finished stints in Juvenile and Family Court as Juvenile Public Defender and as Guardian ad Litem, so I was familiar with the problems that social workers have in keeping up with all of their cases, even in Minnesota. Luis did say that his father lived there and was at work—a big surprise for me because the father had been missing from the home through all of our years of correspondence.

Some months later I found out that the mother was being treated for cancer and that she and the little girl were in the U.S. The father was working as a block layer, at a very low wage. Luis also worked as a block layer part time, and attended high school. PLAN had left the area and had no further connection with him. I tried to find some other organization through which I could continue to help him. No success, but I did get his home mailing address. My bank said that the banks there are so corrupt that it would probably be impossible send anything like a cashier's check and have him get anything from it, so I finally wrote a letter to him and enclosed some Guatemalan currency and my mailing address. Bryan also wrote to Winkler, asking if there was some way that he could help the sister that was there, but got no answer. It seemed that we had lost them, but, about two years later, I was surprised to get a letter from Luis. He had received my letter, and he gave me some account of his life since I had seen him—he was working, not attending any type of school. He said that he was pleased to hear from me, but that he did not want money. I wrote back and, perhaps foolishly, enclosed a little more cash. I never heard from him again. I often wonder about him; he would be about twenty-seven now.

After Bryan and I said our goodbyes to Luis and his sister that day, our "staff" took us to the bus station where we boarded the bus for an hour's ride to Antigua to meet Ray, Steve and Margit. The bus ride (only an hour or so) was memorable. The bus, similar to an old school bus, was jammed to the gunwales with humanity. The lady next to Bryan had three small children. They were incredibly dirty and smelled unbelievably bad as she tried to feed them some unappetizing mess while they crawled all over Bryan and their mother and the floor and seat. The ride brought us an example of a Latin American way of dealing with problems. Their government had foolishly passed a law that busses were not allowed to carry standees. The law created an impossible situation because there were few busses and great need for transportation, so the law was totally ignored except in one respect. As the bus approached the police stations spaced along the highway, the driver let out a shout. Everybody in the aisles then made an elaborate show of trying to bend, squat or stoop so as put themselves below window level and out of sight—something that was totally impossible. The policemen studiously fixed their eyes on some distant cloud as the bus swept by, and then all of the riders joined in a rousing cheer and a hearty laugh as they straightened up again.

By Sunday night we were back in Conacaste among the pigs, chickens and burning garbage. Our second week was similar to the first, except for better star gazing at night. Polaris is close to the northern horizon down there; Orion is nearly overhead, and there is little light pollution in San Conacaste, so the sights in the sky are often magnificent.

We also visited the local elementary school one afternoon, and threw a piñata party for the kids, which was fun, but our greatest pleasures during that week came from the two afternoons that we spent with the Gonzales family, working on their farm. This couple had a virtual army of handsome sons and daughters, teen-aged and under, who met us. They divided themselves among us so that each of us had an instructor-partner for the job in the fields. The kids were friendly and chatty; they talked as we all worked so there were multiple Spanish-English lessons in progress, and picture taking at the end. Their father had been working apart from us in another field. He came over to visit when we finished, and built a little fire as we talked. When that got going he went into the field and pulled some ears of corn. He threw these right into the fire for a while, raked them out and rolled them around, then put them back onto the hot coals. When he pulled them out again he passed them around with lime and salt. It was delicious—the green husks create a steam cooker within each ear, and the corn cooks beautifully. "Country style," he said. It was the only English I heard him speak.

Thinking back on that Guatemala journey, I always seem to come back to the contrasts, and especially to the contrast between the Gonzales family and another man that I saw frequently. I don't know what the future held for those Gonzales kids, but at the time we saw them the family and their life would almost be the envy of suburban America—they were so attractive, so well-spoken, so happy, so smart, so busy.

The other image is of the man I saw frequently but never met. He was a mystery that I should have looked into but, I am sorry to say, did not. Each evening he would come along a little footpath near our site. He wore black, tattered garments and appeared to be very dirty. Always, he came shuffling along, bent nearly double under the weight of a large bundle of sticks on his back. Where he got the sticks, or where he was going with them, I can't imagine. He seemed to be an anachronism—a throwback to an ancient time when men were serfs and life was nothing. There was no one else like that in San Conacaste, and I never saw him have any sort of contact with any other human being. Perhaps he was mentally ill; I don't know. But I still see him, shuffling, dragging, staggering along, black and soiled, bent over so far that his hands could almost have reached the ground if they had not been clutched at his breast holding the threadbare cords that bound the outsized bundle of sticks to his back.

A Cosmic Villanelle

Astronomers say that the Great Spiral Galaxy in Andromeda is on a collision course with the Milky Way.

Andromeda is coming here
to merge with our own Milky Way.
The universe is passing queer.

The stars above will wheel and veer,
a billion suns in grand melee.
Andromeda is coming here.

Orion kissing Draco's ear,
Virgo's hair in disarray.
The universe is passing queer.

With Heaven maybe moving near,
Satan's wife could lose her way.
Andromeda is coming here.

An end to evil, pain, and fear.
The crap excised from DNA.
The universe is passing queer.

Galaxies twining may, just may
gain back what Adam pissed away.
Andromeda is coming here.
The universe is passing queer.

A Cosmic Villanelle was originally published by Artword Quarterly (Fall 1999, No. 18, and was nominated for the Pushcart Prize XXV anthology.

I Think He Died Last Year

"Is Art still living?" LaVerne asked.

"Gosh, I'm not sure. It seems to me that he died. Jerry, do you know? Did Art Schmidt die?"

"I dunno. If he didn't, he will. Ask Sam."

"Yes," Sam answered. "He died a couple of years ago. Don't you remember, he came in here one day with his skin all yellow, and then about a week later we heard he was dead."

"Yeah, I guess that's right. He always was kind of stubborn. They talk about one time away back when his dad was still living. They had a balky mule and it stopped out in the field late one afternoon when Art was cultivating corn. He sat there on the cultivator all night until the sun came up and the mule finally gave in and decided to move. Art finished the round and made one more before he came in for breakfast."

"Sounds like bullshit," I said.

"No, no, it really happened. Just ask Ernie; he lived neighbors to them. He'll tell you all about it."

"He was a hard worker," said Sam. "And a good guy, too. I always got a kick out of him. He came up north fishing with us a couple of times, years ago. Didn't know diddly about fishing, but he was good around the camp and liked to talk if you once got him going."

"Yeah, I know he did a lot for his sister and her kids when they were in trouble," put in LaVerne. "Not many people knew anything about that."

A lot of the conversation at the Oasis is about dead people. This is not surprising, once you think about it. Most of us who congregate there are eighty or so and, truth to tell, most of the people we know are dead. For everyone, not just for us, some people we knew when we were young will always be dominant figures in our psyche—our parents, grandparents, the mother-in-law—our aunts and uncles, some neighbors. For the cluster of geezers on the stools at the Oasis counter, these prominent individuals are all figures of the past, but their personalities still loom large in our reckoning. Many of the people we discuss have been gone for thirty years or more.

Equally dead are many of our brothers and sisters, wives, cousins, co-workers, classmates, army friends, and drinking buddies. We recall them all fondly, as we do some of our associations with them, so it's no wonder that we talk about them.

Others may see this seeming preoccupation with the dead as morbid, but it is not. Rather, it is a celebration of those lives— lives that touched us in some way—often in many ways. It is, in fact, often a better celebration of those lives than was the funeral that consigned them to the grave—and our celebration goes on for years. Most of us spend a lot of time alone now, so we have time to think back upon various incidents, and then make those incidents come to life again at the Oasis.

While we don't really have any suggestions for improving the formal funeral, we do note its defects—it tends to be a stilted, generic exercise where some stranger reads a bunch of biblical passages deemed suitable for such occasions while everyone else sits around self consciously in their good clothes, wondering how to act. Mark Twain, of course, knew how to act, even in such trying circumstances, so in *Letters from the Earth*, he left a list of instructions for the rest of us: "If the official hopes expressed concerning the person in whose honor the entertainment is given are known by you to be oversized, let it pass—do not interrupt." And, "At the moving passages, be moved—but only according to your degree of intimacy with . . . When a blood relative sobs, an intimate friend should choke up, a distant acquaintance should sigh, a stranger should merely fumble sympathetically with his handkerchief."

He closes his list with a final, sound, snippet: "Do not bring your dog."

At the Oasis, the line between the living and the dead tends to blur a little. Art, while living, is important to us, even if we haven't seen him for several years. So if we've forgotten that he died, it's much the same as if he had not. He's still just as important to us, and what we don't know doesn't really matter. He's almost equally alive to us either way. The things that we know him for are still alive. And that makes us feel good because it means, in a way, that we may still be alive after we die too.

So if you happen to see one of us sitting alone on a park bench, rheumy eyes staring absently at the tips of our toes, do not imagine that this lassitude is a sign of a vacant mind. Our mind is busy, and we need this solitude to allow it to work. We are reliving the day they delivered the new 1937 Ford to the farm, and took away the old Pontiac and the three horses that Dad had traded for it—reliving the day and getting all of the details straight again. And if you will stop in at the Oasis for breakfast some morning, you may hear all about it. Dad and those horses will come to life again, and you can share the first ride we took in the Ford—the memorable ride where Dad, by mistake, drove all the way to Madison in second gear while we commented on how smooth and effortless this was compared to plugging along in the old Pontiac.

Divorce Court

The courtroom's empty as the moon.
Words echo through its dim recesses.
ivory chairs in the jury box
gleam like fangs in the jaw of a yawning wolf.

The parties sit at counsel table
with sweaty palms and gritted teeth.
They want to tell. It's why they came.
What he said to her–and how she felt.

The judge has heard this all before.
The court reporter takes it down,
but doesn't really hear it said.
The clerk has stamped the affidavits.
The lawyers feign a solemn mein.

But this deed was done
before the gavel ever fell.

The stipulation–signed and dated,
set to be read into the record.
The child support, asset division,
the mortgage payment, visitation.
The pension fund, attorney's fees,
the skids are greased on all of these.

But twenty years – to end like this,
here where no one gives a rip.
She wants to talk, to justify.
She wants assurance. She wants to cry.
He's forlorn too, he'll miss his kids.
Wants to explain how hard he worked,
wants to recount some things she did.

It's all worked out but, Oh! what's missing.
There ought to be someone to listen.

Faces of Solitude

All of the cowboy movie stars sang it, but Gene Autry did it the best. *You don't know what lonesome is 'till you get to a'herding cows.* Except, of course, the animals were "caows" and the line was rendered in a plaintive wail that could set the dogs to howling. Even so, what it says is true. I know. Farmers spend a lot of time alone, but usually in some busy, or even strenuous activity. Herding cows is slow.

In the years when I was about ten to twelve, herding cows was my job for most of the summer. This was South Dakota during the dry years of the 1930s, and, without rain, our pasture wasn't adequate to feed our cattle, so my job was to take them out on the road and herd them where they could graze on the grass that grew in the ditches.

Each morning except Sunday, about eight, after the cows were milked and we had finished breakfast, I could be seen bridling Teddy, my pony, opening the barnyard gate, and moving off down the driveway and up the road to the east with a herd of twenty or thirty cows. They were docile enough, and Teddy knew the drill well, so it was easy for me to do.

There were unwritten laws about where to take your cows, because other farmers might be doing the same thing. Generally speaking, you stuck to roads that bordered your own farm, or to roads that neither of the adjoining farmers used for grazing. Also, if at all possible, you stuck to roads where the adjoining fields were fenced—it made the job a lot easier.

Once in place, the cattle spread themselves out along the ditches on both sides of the road, and Teddy and I settled down to a long morning in the hot Dakota sun. Trees were scarce. Some days a car or two might come by, but usually there were none. We watched the shadows of fence posts to judge the time, and roused our charges up and moved them home as noon approached.

62 – At the Oasis

Our job ended in mid August. After the oats crop had been cut, shocked, and threshed, the cattle were turned into the fields of oats stubble, where they became gleaners, prospered, and increased their production of milk. The advent of August made me happy because I had not yet developed an aptitude for the amount of solitude involved in herding cows. Those cow-herding days seemed interminable. I'm surprised now that I didn't find something more productive to do. I could have read books, or whittled, or learned to knit, or something. But I didn't. We (Teddy and I) just stood around, or I lay on his back. He was big for a pony—all black except for a white star on his forehead, and my constant companion. We performed our meager duties, and sat some more and hated it as the hours crawled.

Now, so many years later, my attitude about solitude has changed—I often seem to seek solitude, or to find it productive when circumstances force it upon me. Solitude, in my experience, allows me to think. In fact, as others have pointed out, it seems to be almost essential to that process. For many, certainly for me, and perhaps for everyone, the ability to think is the essence of being human. In a way, the concept of thinking about the world burst upon me one day when I was nine years old and chanced upon, in my sister's high school textbook, an explanation of the layout of the solar system. I was astonished—I still feel the shock of that moment, and I read with rapt attention. I had never dreamt of such a thing. The awe and joy of science and math, revealed to me that day, have never left, and I think this goes some distance toward explaining my need for the solitude needed for study. Without the fascination of mathematics, my life would have been but a shadow of what I have known, and I'm not even very good at it. I'm not really trained in math, beyond the utilitarian aspects of it that are useful in engineering. I have an interest in higher mathematics, but it is the interest of an enthusiastic amateur. I feel sorry for those who have never experienced this all-consuming enchantment, and for the fact that they have no concept of what it could be for them. Robert Oppenheimer, the famous American physicist who headed the team that developed the atomic bomb, had a quip about it. "Doing mathematics has something in common with sex," he said. "Both activities have important practical applications, but that is not, generally speaking, why people participate in them."

A few years ago I became interested in an ancient math problem—The Pythagorean Theorem. As Pythagoras deduced, and as everyone now knows: In any right triangle, the square of the length of the hypotenuse is equal to the sum of the squares of the lengths of the other two sides. If, for example, the two shorter sides are 4 and 5 inches long respectively, then $16 + 25 = 41$, and so the length of the hypotenuse is the square root of 41, or about 6.483 inches.

But are there right triangles where the lengths of all three sides are whole numbers? Well, yes. Every carpenter knows of one such solution, $3^2 + 4^2 = 5^2$ $(9+16=25)$. He uses this knowledge routinely to make square corners. So (3,4,5) is a solution. Are there other solutions, and, if so, how does one find them? That is the problem.

Who cares? Well, it turns out that a lot of people do, or at least that a lot of people care about the solution of more complex problems of this kind—problems where the answers must be whole numbers. A major part of the work of modern mathematicians goes into such problems. This situation seems to arise from the quantum nature of our world, which is to say that if we look closely enough, everything seems to be discrete; nothing is continuous. When it comes to atoms, for example, you may have 1 atom, or 2 atoms, or possibly 3,748, 367 atoms, but not 3 ½ atoms. Normally, there is no such thing as half an atom, and to deal with atoms, we need a branch of mathematics where the answers are restricted to whole numbers. This restriction applies not only to atoms, but to many other concepts, such as modes of resonance. So the mathematics of whole numbers is vital to the scientists who are trying to invent and build the things we use.

But that gets into the practical applications. As Oppy said, for the mathematician, the real lure is in the problem itself, not in its application. Oh, of course, it's convenient to be paid, and most jobs that pay deal with applications, but a problem can have an application and still be interesting. It is hard to overstate the fascination of the problem as such. Mathematics engages the mind in much the same way that puzzles do, so it is a recreation as well as a scientific tool.

My children are married, and have families of their own. Their spouses also have, of course, parents, brothers, sisters, aunts, uncles, and cousins. For us, as for many families, this raises the issue of how to celebrate Christmas and other holidays where families want to be together. In our case, it has worked out that we normally get together on Christmas Eve to have dinner and a few drinks, to enjoy the grandchildren, to exchange gifts, and to tell stories, talk, and whoop it up generally. Then the kids and their families are free to spend Christmas Day with the in-laws.

So after a family Christmas Eve celebration a few years back, I was alone on the following day. After cleaning up the debris from the party, I started working on the problem above—the problem of finding whole-number solutions to the Pythagorean Equation. In many ways, it was the best Christmas I have ever spent. I sat alone at my desk and computer in a room of my big, old farmhouse, utterly absorbed, from midmorning until well past midnight, hardly even stopping to eat.

I didn't finish solving my problem that day, but I eventually did, several months later, and then I could toy with solutions that involved numbers up into the millions and billions. The next solution after (3,4,5) was (5,12,13) or 25 + 144 = 169. A success like this was unusual for me; failure with such problems was my usual mode. Ecstatic, I wrote up my solution and sent it to several university math departments for comment. I had assumed from the beginning that, if such a basic problem had a solution, it must have been discovered long ago, perhaps by Fermat, perhaps even back in ancient times. But I had studiously avoided looking in books for the answer—that would have been like cheating at solitaire. I cared more about doing it than I cared about the answer.

A math professor at ISU in Ames was particularly helpful. He went over my work in some detail, gave me references, and wrote me a nice letter. It turned out that I had independently retraced the steps of an ancient mathematician, Diophantus of Alexandria, whose life had salvaged some of the lost glory of Greece and Rome during the twilight of paganism in the third century A.D. It was a great feeling for me, like a touching of hands across the millennia. I felt a kinship, as if he and I, in the shadows of the Sphinx and the Pyramids (which were already ancient in his time) had worked this out together. I thought of Galileo and Kepler, who corresponded with each other 1300 years later as they worked out the true nature of the solar system.

In ancient times, due to the vagaries of war, educated men were sometimes forced into slavery and labored as academics for their captors. Plato himself was a slave briefly until ransomed. So I think Diophantus probably had slaves to help him do some tedious and mundane calculations that are involved in developing the answer and checking it out. I didn't have any slaves, but I had a computer that could crunch numbers faster than the most canny slave, so I thought we were more or less even on this score. Except for these calculations, which are secondary to the main work of finding the solutions, my computer was of very little help to me. Potentially, of course, I had a huge advantage over Diophantus in that I could have looked up the answer in a Theory of Numbers textbook, and he couldn't have—but I didn't, and that has made all the difference.

Why are such problems so interesting? Undoubtedly, part of the fascination of all puzzle solving is ego based, but it seems to me that something more is involved too—that puzzles get us outside of ourselves, that we have some innate interest in problems for their own sake. Many human blessings are shared with a number of animals. We are curious, but the curiosity of cats, and its dire consequences, is proverbial. We can do puzzles, but some horses are notorious for their ability to puzzle out ways to open gates and escape confinement. We have a sense of satisfaction for having done something well, or something worthwhile. Perhaps animals have this too, I don't know. I wonder if a winning racehorse, headed toward its stall, says to itself, "Well, I done good." And if it does, I wonder how the horse in second place feels about it.

But I just don't think horses or cats are interested in puzzles unless they see some potential for a tangible payoff. I suspect that the love of puzzles for their own sake is a human characteristic—perhaps even an essential one. I don't think a cat would be interested in doing mathematics just for the joy of doing it, even if it knew how.

More recently I became aware of another unexpected advantage of solitude. I have long enjoyed writing, and so I decided to try to learn more about it by getting myself enrolled at Mankato State University as a graduate student in English with a specialty in creative writing, and working toward a degree. The university is some distance from my home, so it takes me two or three hours to drive there. Although I finished the work and was awarded the MFA degree several years ago, I still go there sometimes to audit a class or to attend a reading. The route I travel is a "blue highways" route, with little traffic, so the trips are quite relaxed. But I spend a lot of time alone, behind the wheel, going back and forth.

People ask me, and I ask myself—why do I do this? There are closer places I could go. Part of the answer is that I feel at home at Mankato—I know the faculty, I know the library, I like it there. Another part is that most of the drive to Mankato is rural; I don't have the white-knuckle feeling that plagues me in city traffic.

But, I have come to realize, there is another reason—a reason that is perhaps more important than either of these. The fact is that I do much, perhaps the most important part, of my writing while I am driving along on these trips.

I have a radio in my car. It came with the car, but I almost never use it. My grandchildren, if they have occasion to be passengers in my car, tend to become impatient with me when they realize that I don't actually know how to operate the radio, despite the fact that I've had the car for more than two years. But the car is quiet during my trips to Mankato, and my mind is on the English Department and the literary world anyway, so it is an excellent time to write.

Not that I use pencil and paper or tap text into my laptop as I'm going down the road. I don't drive nearly well enough to be able to do anything like that. Some have suggested that I should carry a tape recorder, wear a head mike, and talk into it as I go. But that is wrong, and would destroy the effectiveness of those sessions.

The reason those sessions work so well is precisely because I am unhampered by any need to record my thoughts. The mind can be lightning fast—it is capable of processing a dozen thoughts, or of reprocessing one thought into a dozen variations, in the time it would take to speak it or to write it down. Of course, those thoughts also have something in common with dreams—like dreams, they can vanish from the conscious mind within seconds. But the good ones leave some sort of a dim track inside, and when I again fall to mulling things over at another time, my mind tends to return to the same ideas it has explored before. The good thoughts are retraced, and their dim tracks become deeper ruts in my conscious or unconscious mind. Finally, perhaps months later, and perhaps late at night while I sit at my desk hunched over my keyboard, my mind, largely of its own accord, begins to again race through those tangled, well-worn ruts, and the ideas appear on paper.

So, at least for me, the solitude of the trip is important, perhaps essential. It may well be that the time spent in the car, going and coming, helps my writing more than the speaker I went to hear does. It is hard to imagine another activity that enforces solitude as rigorously as driving a car does. One simply cannot turn aside for a few minutes to rearrange the magazines on the coffee table, or to call about a dental appointment, or to make the bed.

There are, of course, other routes to solitude. Some people have a happy capacity for forcing it upon themselves, whether alone or in the midst of others. This trait is conducive to deep thought for them, although it can be disconcerting for those around them. Robert Oppenheimer (mentioned above) was such a man. I can't personally vouch for this story about him, but it is often told:

Before the facilities at Los Alamos were ready to be occupied, Oppenheimer worked out of a laboratory at a university in California. To get to work each morning he had to drive across a toll bridge, and had to stop at a tollgate to hand the attendant a dollar bill. He seemed to do this automatically, without ever taking his mind off of whatever he was thinking about.

At Los Alamos, of course, security was a high priority, and the whole installation was heavily guarded. Germany and Japan were both known to have competing atomic projects, and the lives of thousands, or perhaps millions, of people were at stake. For General Leslie Groves, the commander of the installation, security was paramount. Many of the scientists and other civilian workers lived off post, and had to show their badges and be checked in through the gates each morning. The leading scientists, like Oppenheimer, were expected to lead by example. Nobody was to be allowed to go through the gate without stopping and showing his badge. Otherwise it would become a game of who was famous enough to be excused, and Groves couldn't afford games.

68 – At the Oasis

Oppenheimer knew all of this, and had agreed completely when Groves talked with him about it. The problem was—he always forgot. Lost in thought, he would drive up to the gate; pass by all of the signs and sentries standing there, and go on to his office. The sentries knew full well who he was, so there was no actual danger, but he was setting a terrible example. After several recurrences of this were reported to Groves, he called the sentries and their commanders to his office and set up a stringent response. The next time it happened, a sentry was to fire a shot from his rifle into the road in front of Oppy's car. The stage was set.

And sure enough, the very next morning, it happened again. Oppenheimer drove slowly through the gate, his brow furrowed, his gaze absently on the road, and his lips working silently as he explored some problem in nuclear fission. The sentry team was ready, with a man in position ready to fire, and, upon signal, he did so. The gravel and blacktop in front of the car spurted from the impact, pebbles flew, and the bullet ricocheted off into the distance with a satisfying whine.

Oppenheimer stopped, put his car into reverse, backed up to where the sentry stood, handed him a dollar bill, and drove on.

A prime example of an isolation that occurs involuntarily is the isolation that often comes, unbidden, with old age. When the ears and eyes begin to fail it is hard to keep track of what is going on, or to be a part of it. Others become impatient, and are apt to snort something about hearing aids, or getting your glasses changed, so the older person withdraws from abrasive contacts which he can make nothing of. To his surprise, he often finds that it really makes very little difference whether he can hear what is being said or not—there is an enormous redundancy and predictability to most talk, and catching a few words is often enough. But he does miss some content too, and worse, he begins to quit listening.

Also, when life is mostly behind rather than ahead, it is hard to maintain the same interest in some of its activities. These withdrawals of the elderly are not necessarily seen as positive developments, but they do have a bright side. I know many older people and they are, as a class, more reflective than their younger counterparts. Tradition regards the elder as being wise, but I wonder if he really is. It may only be that, being necessarily somewhat detached from life, he is inclined to speak of it in more general terms, and this makes him seem wise.

Still another route to solitude sometimes—not always, but sometimes—beckons to me strangely. A new experience—life behind bars. Escape, I suppose; escape into prison. Imagine the peace. A library, a computer, an exercise yard. Probably everything I need to be able to read and write. What better place could there be for the man who can't say no? The perfect excuse for everything. Sorry, I'd like to help, or to keep you company, but they won't allow me to leave here.

Friends have ridiculed me about this idea. "If you knew what jail was like," they say, "you'd sing another tune." But they misunderstand on a couple of counts. To some limited extent, I do know what jail is like. I still remember, as a young man of seventeen, and a migrant farm laborer in the Red River Valley of North Dakota and Minnesota, that I once had to visit the drunk tank of the jail in East Grand Forks to rescue Olaf Ramsey, an errant companion. Ole and Sverre Gulstine, each about twelve years my senior, had sort of adopted me, so we were a trio. We spent most of our time in the fields, picking potatoes or threshing wheat, but there were also some rainy day stretches in town where they tried, with little success, to introduce me to drinking, and a couple of times when they undertook, with even less success, to interest me in prostitutes. I don't know how old they were, but they seemed like older ladies to me at the time.

It is true that it would have been difficult for any writer to turn out good work in that jail. The large cell was filled with the stench of urine and vomit, with the drunken babbling of a few of the guests, and with the anger or resignation of others who had to smell and listen while they waited for release. Ole was happy to see us, and the Forks Finest, having bigger fish to fry, were glad to get themselves shet of him, so our mission was an undoubted success.

I have also visited clients in our local county jail. Conditions there were less draconian, and the inmates were afforded a good deal of solitude, but they had few facilities and seemed to live as transients, waiting for bail or release, or for the end of a short sentence. For a writer, I think, "getting his shit together" in such a setting would be difficult.

But these are jails. Prison has a strong connotation of permanence. When I say prison I have in mind something more akin to the Birdman of Alcatraz, Robert Stroud.

Stroud not only wrote two books during his long years in prison; he also did the original research upon which his books were based. His subject was the diseases of canaries. He raised nearly 300 of them in his cell, and his scientific observations of them also helped later research on the species. Ever resourceful, Stroud was once caught using a still that he had constructed from his canary gear.

There also are, and have been, others who took advantage of the solitude of prison life to write. They have, in fact, a literary journal of their own. *Corrections: A Literary Journal* even publishes some of their work on the web.

Picture the luxury of an existence like Stroud's—scads of available time. Days, weeks on end, day and night, hour after hour. A whole busy Tuesday, pouring over a manuscript to remove a single comma. Magnificent, even if I put it back in on Wednesday. Thursday would be ahead, and Friday. Plenty of time to write more then—or on Saturday night! I've always been creative on Saturday night. Maybe I should read on Thursday instead, there's so much to keep up with. And I must get back to Baudelaire to help him explore his world of locks and compartments, "replete, like every civilized soul, with secrets."

This French poet bemoaned, and recounted in detail, the trivia that consumed his waking hours. "Alone at last!" he says at one o'clock in the morning as he double locks his door behind him and asks for the grace to produce some beautiful passages of poetry in the few hours of silence, if not repose, ahead. "At last!" he says, "the tyranny of the human face has vanished."

Baudelaire tells of a dream in which the routine of daily life had become an enormous Chimera, heavy as a sack of coal, which each traveler carried on his back while it hugged and clutched at him. Perhaps the chimera was a familiar figure in his day (1821–1867), but most of us now need to resort to a dictionary to find it to be a mythical, dragon-like beast. Curiously, Baudelaire's travelers did not seem to resent the burdensome load that bent them double—rather, they seemed to regard it as an essential part of themselves.

Well, this traveler has often resented the ravening beast wrapped around his neck and stuck to his back—it is not an essential part of me. Legions of friends lie, already, in graveyards strewn from Anzio to Sioux Falls. Am I obliged to join them without ever having time to explore the literary feast that separates us from animals, or attempting to add my crumb to it?

It is thoughts and questions like these that drive my occasional outbursts where I picture prison life as a way to get away from people, and maybe not so bad. Is this selfish, I ask myself. Can't they talk to each other about salad dressing ingredients and football? Must I sit and keep them company while days and years slip into oblivion, foregoing my chance to snatch a moment from eternity? Bunkum. Hold open the sally port, jailer. Wait for me.

But, of course, I only feel that way sometimes—and any serious consideration of the idea reveals some problems inherent in it. How, for example, would one go about getting admitted to a prison? It costs the taxpayers a lot of money to keep a prisoner, and so the government is probably not interested in volunteers. Stroud, a pimp, got in originally by murdering, and then robbing, a customer who didn't pay his prostitute, and stayed by virtue of other violent acts he performed as a prisoner. Finally, before Alcatraz, he stabbed a guard to death in front of eleven hundred inmates in the prison mess hall at Leavenworth. I really could not, for many reasons, do anything like that regardless of how desperate I might be for solitude. What would my grandchildren think?

And, actually, my craving for solitude only consumes me intermittently. At other times I have a strong need for human companionship. If I were in prison I would be excluded, for example, from our breakfast coffee sessions on the stools along the counter at the Oasis Café. And I would miss the conversations we have there, even the ones where the talk is mostly about mundane things like the weather or some feature of the red pickup that Ernie drives. Chaucer and Shakespeare were not above mixing gossip with their famous ideas about the world they lived in, and neither am I. And, anyway, to some extent I feel a duty, a social obligation, to listen. Other people sometimes need someone to listen to them. A trace of the social behavior that characterizes ants and bees is present in all of us. Sometimes it's nice to be able to talk with people whether you learn anything from the conversation or not—and, every so often, you do.

So, although I have changed, I guess I also still retain some vestige of the state of mind that possessed me when Teddy and I passed those interminable summer days along an empty road with placid cows that made no demand upon us for companionship.

A *Private Goodbye*

Originally published:
The Portland Review
Volume 49, No. 1
FALL/WINTER 2001

Years have passed, but in my mind I'm back there again today, as I often am–hurrying into her room, sitting in the chair beside her bed.

Two weeks had made a melancholy difference, I could see that. She had grown even thinner, if such a thing was possible. She was asleep or unconscious, and her head was lying there on the pillow like a wasted, delicate flower. The last time I was here she made a fuss about wanting to get her teeth in and her glasses on for me. "You haven't worn these for quite a while, Mary," the nurse had said, helping her. I wondered if she had worn the glasses since; they were lying in their case on the table by the bed.

The place was quiet, although it wasn't eight o'clock yet; the silence was seldom broken, and then only by quick, quiet footsteps and a flash of white as the night nurse hurried by the open door. This Madison, South Dakota, small town hospital didn't draw many visitors on weekday winter evenings in 1971—most people came in the afternoon. I had left work in the Twin Cities a few minutes early to get to the airport and catch a 5:40 plane to Sioux Falls. The flight was less than an hour, and the rental car was ready when I got there, so I was on my way to Madison by seven o'clock.

I sat and watched Mother, and held her hand for half an hour or so, hoping there would be a chance for us to talk, probably for the last time. But she didn't stir. Gradually, the past that I shared with her began to assume a reality that it usually no longer had for me.

I was glad to see that past coming back so vividly—It allowed my mother to resume her true identity, to escape from being this silent, shriveled creature, alone on a hospital bed. My father had died six years earlier, and my brothers and sister also had families and jobs to attend to in other parts of the country. As Mother's cancer had grown worse, the past months had seen a series of hurried trips home for all of us, but still, she was often alone. Those months had been hard for her—doubly hard after an eventful life, I thought.

I was forty-seven then. It had already been nearly thirty years since I had lived in Dakota, and our busy life in Minnesota consumed all of my attention most of the time. We were busy at the 3M lab in St. Paul where I worked; the Adjutant General had recently assigned me the responsibility for National Guard units in five cities in Southwestern Minnesota; I had recently remarried following the death of my wife two years earlier, and my kids, in all stages from elementary school to college, were having trouble adapting to a stepmother in the house; and I was serving as chairman of our Township Board of Supervisors, which was in the midst of a rancorous annexation battle with the neighboring City of Stillwater.

But sitting alone with her in that quiet room I saw her again as she had been. I saw her as she marched into our one-room country school to accost our teacher about her practice of forcing us to keep our lunch buckets in the unheated entry way. After that day's work, we no longer had to gnaw on frozen peanut butter sandwiches for lunch.

A good day's work, I mused. The phrase reminded me of Robert Burns and that crowning glory, his poem, "Tam O'Shanter." He wrote it all in one day; in his country it is said to be "the best day's work done in Scotland since Robert the Bruce routed the English invaders at Bannockburn in 1314."

I thought also of an even earlier day in mother's life. I was four or five and we lived on that farm south of Grandma's. It was threshing time, and Mother, although seriously ill, had rushed from the house to snatch my two-year-old brother from the path of a runaway team of horses. And I thought of how she was with her sister, my Aunt Nelle—how they would sit and giggle together like schoolgirls, even in their forties. I almost envy them the childhood they must have had, and that pony of theirs, that "ran like the wind."

These thoughts brought others. Mother with her chickens, how she would croon and sing to them in their own language. And her skill in canning food and putting up meat. One winter day in 1936 we butchered a steer and four hogs, and she made summer sausage, dried beef, smoked ham, delicious canned beef, and homemade laundry soap. That same year, we had racks of bottles of homemade ketchup, something I haven't seen since.

Mother was tall, erect, slender, and prematurely gray when I was a child. Sitting there I remembered her appearance and her persona in public when she led us to church, or took us to Madison, shopping. In those foreign, to me, surroundings, with paved streets, sidewalks, and strangers, she marched along, at home, at ease, imperious. She was so attractive then, so dignified. I was in awe of her. Perhaps it was a holdover from her days as a school teacher.

Eight o'clock had become ten, and still she had not stirred. I walked around the room—stared out of the window. South Dakota stared back with its characteristic quiet; the wind drifted wisps of light snow through the cornfield across the road; there were no people in sight. I noticed a handwritten note, dated two days earlier, on the shelf below the dark and silent TV. It was from my cousin, June, who lived in town, saying that she had been there, and suggesting that we (any visitors) keep in touch by adding to her note. It seemed like a good idea, but I realized later that I had left without doing it.

Eleven o'clock approached, and found me still there, reluctant to leave, even though my flight back was scheduled for sixteen minutes after midnight, and it was nearly forty miles to the airport. Gotta go!

I barely made that "redeye" flight, racing up the deserted ramp and shouting "wait for me" as the flight attendant was closing the gate. She was good natured about it and smiled as she held the door open. "Welcome aboard," she said.

I dozed during the short and nearly empty flight, got my car from the ramp, and was home at 1:45 a.m.—hngry. I fried two eggs for a big sandwich, washed it down with a glass of milk, and headed for bed, aware that 7:00 a.m. would be coming early.

In bed, I pushed sleep away for a few more minutes to reflect upon the night, as I have often reflected upon it since. A sorrowful, humbling experience, strangely made stronger by its isolation. Had my trip been worthwhile? Mother didn't know, and would never know, that I had visited her. In all of this vast world, in fact, there was not another person who even knew I had been there.

Robert Burns came back to my mind–his thoughts when his plow accidentally destroyed the winter nest of the wee mouse. Were his, perhaps silent, remarks of consequence when they occurred to him there in the field that day, or did they become significant only after the world knew them as poetry? He and the mouse were alone on the moor, and the mouse was, surely, uncomprehending. If no one knows, does it matter that it happened? Without external expression, perhaps all of our thoughts and actions are futile, like a radio playing in an empty room, and my trip had been a fool's errand.

But I don't think so. It seems to me that we are changed by what we think or do, and that, late or soon, we change the world. I don't believe in a hereafter. I don't have any vision of Mother in Heaven looking down upon me with approval, or anything like that. I don't think she would be one to fault me anyway.

But I'm glad I went.

The Eternal Quarrel

"He can't prove it."

"Well, she can't disprove it either."

He thinks that the world was created by God—that the universe came into being by an act of creation not unlike that described in Genesis, and that the Garden of Eden was part of this event.

She sees this as so much arrant nonsense, and she wants to prove him wrong. We may want to say that he is entitled to his opinion, and she to hers, but she'll have none of that—she's determined to prove him wrong. She has, in short, taken the burden of proof upon herself.

She would base her case on the fossils; this is the argument that is universally used. The record of the fossils shows clearly that the earth existed, and teemed with life, for hundreds of millions of years before there were men. Obviously, she would say, this evidence is totally inconsistent with the assumption that the earth, and mankind, were created by God as described in Genesis.

But is it really inconsistent? This crucial point of the argument should be examined more closely than it usually is. Let us take a moment to think about a day of creation more carefully. How would it actually have been done? How is God apt to have handled the myriad of details involved?

We might, for example, look again upon the Garden of Eden, and fasten our attention on some small detail of it—the trees, let us say. If Adam had cut one of those trees down and looked at it, would it have had tree rings?

It could have had rings, we don't know. It would have been up to God whether or not to put them there. Certainly we cannot say that those trees would not have had rings. So, since she has the burden of proof, she would have to be able to prove him wrong even under the assumption that there were rings.

In a way, it seems likely that the trees would have had rings—it would make them like all other trees. If it was done that way it wouldn't be necessary to design special "start-up" trees with no rings. But now we are faced with a strange thing—tree rings that give apparent evidence of a past that never was.

The act of creation would not be limited to the Garden of Eden, of course; it would extend to the entire earth, and beyond. More specifically, for example, it would include South Sea Islands with coral atolls. Coral atolls are made of the skeletons of tiny animals deposited over thousands or millions of years. If we dug into an atoll made on the day of creation would we find the skeletons of tiny animals that had apparently been dead for thousands of years? Again, we would have to consider that possibility. It would have been up to God, of course, but that would seem to be the logical way to go about it.

Casting our minds in a slightly different direction, we might consider some live animals. Most of us have seen the way of a goose with her goslings, how she teaches, and they learn the things they need to know to survive in the wild. The memory of those lessons is imprinted, and never leaves the mind of the gosling. Did the grown up goslings that came into being on creation day have, in their minds, the memory of a mother goose that never was? If not, how did they know what to do? Did memories of his "past" crowd the mind of Adam himself? His would have been an unusual human mind indeed if they did not; most of what is in our mind is associated with memory.

God, as the ultimate engineer, could very well have brought the universe "on line" in a steady-state configuration. A power able to do such a thing is so awesome that it is hard to imagine such an event, but that is no argument here. If we can imagine creation in the first place, we can equally well imagine it being done that way.

In other words, if there was a creation, it may well have, and probably did, create an apparent past that had never actually existed. From our perspective now, this artificial past would blend seamlessly into the real past somewhere back behind us, and there would be no way to tell when creation actually occurred. It could have been 6000 years ago as the creationists like to argue. Or, to carry the logic a step further, it could equally well have been at some other time. A power great enough to create stars, galaxies, ants and elephants would have no trouble setting up ten thousand libraries with ten million books and a Dewey decimal system to keep track of them. The story of Genesis, along with Homer's Illiad and Dante's Inferno could all have come into existence together at some later date.

I like to imagine that the world we know actually came into being during the Eisenhower administration. The noticeable lull that pervaded the earth at that time may have had a purpose. In this construct, Hitler and Hiroshima never actually existed, although it doesn't matter to us now that they did not.

The logically flawless argument above is largely due to Phillip Gosse, a 19th century Englishman. With its publication he tried to settle the argument that raged in his day between the evolutionists and the creationists. Unfortunately, it turned out that a settlement on such terms was the last thing that either side wanted. They all turned on him, and he died a bitterly disappointed man. The argument lived on.

Creationists today rely on a variety of devices in their attempts to counteract evidence of an extended past, but they avoid Gosse's argument like a plague. On the other side, Carl Sagan and Jay Gould, like hosts of other scientists, have published outstanding books that show detailed evidence of the development of life through a past that extends back for a billion years. Their books have fine bibliographies, but these bibliographies make no mention of Gosse, and the books ignore the fact that this same detailed evidence of a past could, and probably would, exist even if there had been a day of creation.

Any creator powerful enough to have created the world could easily have created the past too, and would have had good reason to do so. Carl Sagan obviously didn't think it happened that way. I don't think it did either, but no one will ever be able prove that it did or that it did not.

The idea that there is a God, and that God created the world, is an idea that can't be disproved by logic any more than it can be proved. It is an idea beyond logic, an idea based on faith— faith that there was, or faith that there was not, such a creation.

80 – At the Oasis

Since we can never know, except in a faith based way, we might as well stop trying to answer the question for others.

The Day I Met Sam

On a rainy, glum, morning I pulled unto the Oasis Café parking lot and looked around. The lot is, one might say, a bit primitive—full of patches and chuckholes in the ancient blacktop, and shared between the restaurant and a bait shop. The two businesses also share a single building, the only building on the site, which consists of an irregularly-shaped small flat area between the highway and a steep bluff. Large chunks of rock occasionally detach themselves from the bluff and plunge or bounce down to the surface below, so those parts of the lot are avoided by regular patrons.

The edge of the lot that abuts the highway is separated from it by a narrow strip of turf and grass, and there is sufficient room to parallel park a half dozen cars, so my habit is to look for a spot there. In wet weather though, as on that day, water collects along that edge, so I went past, turned around, and pulled in facing north which put the driver's side of the car out of the water and allowed me to dismount and enter the restaurant dry-shod.

Sam happened to be seated alone at the counter, so I took the stool next to him. We exchanged good mornings, as is the custom there, even between strangers, and Kim caught my eye with an inquiring glance from across the room. I nodded in affirmation, which translated into an order for coffee and wheat toast, and searched my mind for a subject upon which I might engage Sam in conversation. I had often seen him there, and heard him addressed as "Sam," but I don't think I had ever actually talked with him. My interest in him was piqued when someone told me that he was Dick Herbert's older brother. I had known Dick for many years—he had once been mayor of Marine-on-St. Croix, a small, historic village about ten miles north of Stillwater. He was also a boat enthusiast and a retired Anderson Window Corp. employee who had turned a hobby into a retirement business. Dick bought, sold, and repaired slot machines nationwide—the old, mechanical, one-armed-bandits, that is. He had no patience for the newer electronic models.

My concern about a topic of conversation with Sam proved to be unnecessary. When Kim brought my toast, Sam slid a little rack of Jelly packages across the counter to me, and then spoke.

"Say, where do you live? I heard someone say that you lived out by Silver Lake."

"Well, yeah, I do. Most of Silver Lake is on my land."

"Well, where's your house then? Jim Parkhurst was a friend of mine and I used to go out to his place a lot. He lived in a new house he built there by the south west corner of the lake."

"Sure. I know the place. A fellow by the name of Jacobson lives there now. Back in the dry years when the lake was low I used to have cattle down there by Jim's house. He had a kid— Mike, I think, who used to come out and talk to us and try to help when we were fixing fence down there. Nice kid. He was only about ten, but I suppose he'd be forty by now."

Sam nodded. "More like fifty, and crippled up. Mike was badly hurt in a fire many years ago. I think he lives out in Montana somewhere."

Owning that lake and farm seemed to do something to validate me in Sam's eyes, so we became friends and talked often after that day. He is very interested in the outdoors—hunting, fishing, or just watching. As a boy, he had spent many days in and around my lake and others like it in our neighborhood. Now over eighty, his activity in such pursuits had slackened, but his interest had not. So we talk of the deer, of the beaver that have become so active in recent years, of the wild turkeys, and about what has become of all of the muskrats that used to be common on Silver Lake and around our area. He knows a lot more about this stuff than I do. I spend a good deal of time in the woods and around the lake, working, and I see all of these animals, and enjoy seeing them, but I have never given them the close attention that enthusiasts like Sam do. Apparently he used to go out to Parkhurst's place and just sit and watch the lake for hours at a time—perhaps observing a group of otters eating a fish. He often tells me things about my own place that I didn't even know. The

Parkhurst house is adjacent to a remote corner of my land, near a tangle of lake, swamp, and tree-covered ridges that I seldom visit.

My own orientation is more farmer than sportsman. My wife and I had both grown up on Dakota farms, so we were happy when we got the chance, so many years ago, to buy this 130 acre place near Stillwater, which put me within easy commuting distance of St. Paul, where I worked at a 3M laboratory. The countryside around us has changed a good deal since then, but the place itself is much the same. The farm, including the farmstead, is old—almost historic. The house and several of the other buildings date back well into the 19th century, so I often wander around the place, muse upon its past, and wish these old walls and rooms and hills and draws could talk and tell me of the things they have seen.

In some ways they can—and do. I have the abstract of title, of course—a record of the owners back to Civil War days. And I have, or did have, neighbors who remembered things about the place from their childhoods in the early part of the 20th century; some of them even lived here and told me where buildings once stood that I can still trace by remnants of the foundations. Beyond that, I get occasional visits from people pursuing their genealogy who come from distant places on little pilgrimages to walk the hills and sit in the rooms that were once home to their great grandparents. And, most of all, I find things. Letters stuffed behind window casings, messages written on the wall beneath the old wallpaper, horseshoes grown into tree stumps, a buried platform scale once used for weighing trucks and wagons, coins, tools, big cisterns in the ground full of water stored there as a fire fighting measure—many such things, often of marvelous workmanship. I think often of these people, these ghosts of the Silver Lake Stock Farm, and wish I could know them in their time better than I do or can.

So I'm glad I met Sam. I'd be glad anyway just to share the other interests we have in common—the army in WWII, his brother, other friends, many things—but the fact that he allows me to see the farm through new eyes and other experiences is priceless.

A Spot in the Woods

Spring creeps into this lonely cove.
The broken stump stands still
gray and ridden with lichen.
Its jagged top grows spongy,
smoothed with years of moss and mold.
Tadpoles and rain puddle in the rotting core,
battalions of ants burrow under the bark,
toadstools thrive in the xylem.
The roots soften
inexorably
below.

Above?
A riot of yellow snapdragons.

Albert's Jacket

I finished wiring the socket, screwed in a bulb and—Voila! Light shown into an area that had been dark for more than forty years, to my knowledge, and probably for a century or more except when occasionally illuminated by the feeble glow of a kerosene lantern.

The spot was in an old barn on my farm. I'm not sure how old that building is—it is of post and beam construction and quite sizeable, 25 by 50 feet. Apparently it was already old when William Kress wrote his name on the back of the big sliding door in 1896. Actually, barn isn't quite the right name for the structure anyway, although the second story does have an overhead track and was apparently used for hay storage. We refer to the building as the Wagon Shed—my kids used to have Halloween parties there. The main floor consists of two rooms—a large one that originally stored racing sulkies used on an adjacent harness racing track, and a smaller one that may have been an office or shop—I use it as a summer office, a nice place to write. The office is served by a large brick chimney that starts in the basement and towers well above the high, peaked roof. The chimney contains two flues; one flue serves the main floor—the other, the basement. The flue that serves the basement is clean of soot on the inside and has apparently never been used. At one time the site also included a large, attached horse barn. It is gone now, although I am still plagued by remnants of its stone foundation in the yard.

The basement gives the appearance of never having been used for much of anything. It is all one large room surrounded by stone walls of excellent construction and roofed by the floor of the main level, which is constructed of three inch thick planks supported on 6 by 14 inch wooden stringers which span the width of the building. Four ground level basement windows admit some feeble illumination, but the whole basement is semi-dark, even on a bright day.

Enclosed stairs lead from the office to the upper level, and access to the basement is from a small closet built under those stairs. From there, another set of stairs leads down through an opening in the floor to the dimly lit basement. With the door closed, the closet itself was almost completely dark, and it was here that I had decided, at long last, to wire a socket and put in a light bulb.

I had lived here for forty years, but this newfound radiance revealed something I had not noticed before. At the far end of the opening in the floor, facing me as I descended the stairs down into the basement, was a ledge, perhaps three feet deep and three feet wide, covered with dirt and old, musty straw. Some weeks later, seized by an impulse to be orderly, I armed myself with a rake and a push broom and set about cleaning off this ledge. It proved to harbor several objects in addition to the old straw and dirt, so I set these aside for later examination.

My loot consisted of the skull of an animal, three bottles, and a denim jacket. I judged the animal to be a weasel, though I wasn't sure. It adorns my desk today, awaiting identification by some passing zoologist. One bottle is a beer bottle; it bears an elaborate trademark molded into the brown glass—Jung BR'G. CO., MILWAUKEE. Google reveals it to be of 1904 vintage. The second bottle looks like it may have held vanilla extract for the kitchen. It says McCONNON'S, WINONA. The third one is broken, incomplete, and seems to be more primitive. It has a number, 29, on the bottom and, in large letters on the side "Patent, Nov 30th, 1858." I should do more research on all three.

But the object that interested me the most was the once blue denim jacket. It dates from a time when denim had nothing to do with fashion. Denim was a cheap, durable fabric used in vast quantities to make work overalls and jackets for men. Thus it was in my youth, and for many years before that. These jackets, which were hip length, buttoned down the front, and had external patch pockets, made no pretext to style beyond, perhaps, the corduroy collar that adorned some models and did feel good when turned up around your neck on cold, windy days.

This particular jacket was worn far beyond anything that one would see on the street today. Patches covered its patches, and still unpatched holes riddled its elbows. Pockets were ripped and torn, bottomless, or missing entirely and replaced with patches cut from discarded overalls. Only one of the original metal buttons remained on the front, others were missing entirely or had been replaced with a variety of mismatched substitutes. The buttonholes were frayed, ragged, stretched out of shape, or torn completely asunder. The one remaining metal button on the front bore the label, KLINK, and a smaller metal button on a cuff said Klink, St. Paul. The jacket was, is, much too small for me. Its owner was a man of small stature. Someone suggested that it could have belonged to a boy, but I was not deceived. Boy's jackets get ripped, torn, mangled, lost, or outgrown, but they never reach the exquisite state of wear that characterizes this garment. This jacket, almost certainly, belonged to a hired man. I call him Albert.

Today we are, for good reason, critical of the lot that fell to our great grandmothers. They lived in a male dominated world, it is said, underpaid, ignored, and discriminated against. And often they did. But we should also remember that many, perhaps most, men occupied an even lower niche in that society. In rural America, which was most of America then, the hired man personifies the lowly denizens of that niche.

For those who care to look, the hired man can be found in our literature. Robert Frost, writing in 1914, calls him Silas, and devotes an entire long poem to him ("The Death of the Hired Man"). William Maxwell refers to him as Victor Jensen, but he is the same person, a man who had no life except the hay he pitched or the cows he milked, day after day, for someone else. Once a month Victor went into town and drank himself into such a stupor that he had to be hauled home a day or two later to dry out and start again. The hired man was often more a creature of the barn than of the house, as much another beast of burden as a man. Some farmers treated him kindly; others did not. Usually, those who treated him kindly treated their horses and cows well too.

Typically, the hired man was of a grizzled, indeterminate age—scarred, bent, and inarticulate. He became a hired man after being a child, and remained one until he died. By then, no one knew where he had come from.

Albert (no one ever called him Al) was, in many ways, such a man—but there were differences too. For one thing, Albert did not drink. The lack of whiskey bottles on the ledge gives mute testimony to that. So even the surcease of narcotic anesthesia, and the false camaraderie of the saloon, were unavailable to him. Albert faced each day alone.

Who's hired man was he, anyway? In 1961 I received a letter from Anna Sexton, an old lady in California who had come to my place with her family in 1896 as a young girl, and had lived here until about 1918. Much of what I know about this place in the old days comes from her. When Sextons left, the place was purchased by the Heifort family who lived here until 1938, when middle daughter, Mabel, married Rudy Ulrich. At that point Mabel and Rudy took over the farm and lived here until shortly before I bought it in 1960. My friend, Fritz Voelker (dead now), who was, in his younger days, Rudy's hired man, was too big to have worn the jacket, so it predates 1938. Heifort descendants are still around and known to me. They were a large family of working farmers who were unlikely to have had need for a permanent hired man. But August Sexton was a business man from Stillwater, and a sort of a Country Gentleman, so Albert undoubtedly worked for the Sextons and was here sometime during the period 1896-1918.

Albert was a small man, of slight build, and timid. He was by no means able to do all of the heavy work that the farm demanded, so the Sextons often had other hired men too from time to time, and hired girls as well, but Albert was permanent. He was one of the family, in a sense, although he certainly was not treated as such. The Sexton house was large, and Albert was allowed to use a small, upstairs bedroom in the winter, but for most of the year he bunked in the Wagon Shed, as did other hired men. By then the racetrack was defunct, so the building was available. Albert usually had to depend on the hired girls for meals, laundry, and whatever other meager services he was provided, but the girls regarded themselves as above him in the pecking order and were frequently scornful of him, so he was often reduced to the role of supplicant. Sometimes he would have to appeal to Mrs. Sexton, who he addressed as "Missus," to get the reluctant girl to patch his jacket, and the ragged nature of her work, on view today, reflects her silent revenge.

Albert was happiest, or at least his unhappiness was at a minimum, in the winter, when he was usually the only hired man there. He was busy all day, milking the cows, feeding them, cleaning out the barn, and caring for the horses and other

animals—his only friends, it seemed. He also had to harness a
team and hitch them to the bobsled to haul wood for the fires in
the house, and was occasionally called upon to use this same
vehicle to transport one or another of the Sexton children to town
or to a neighbor's house. He often ate with the family in the winter,
and at night he was accorded a seat with them in the parlor. His
chair was back in a dark corner against the wall to the right of the
stove, but it was warm there, and Mr. Sexton would sometimes
engage him in short conversations about the state of the hay in the
barn, or the condition of the runners on the bobsled. Best of all,
once in a while, one of the Sexton children would come and stand
at his knee with a doll or toy. The children were awed by the fact
that Albert didn't know how to read, and would sometimes bring
pictures and words to him to investigate this strange phenomena.

During most of the year, however, Albert was consumed by
his timidness, and by a feeling of inferiority because he could not
do heavy work like the other hired men, nor participate in their
loud, bold, and earthy talk. He slunk around, an object of derision,
anxious to be alone. His greatest accomplishment came when he
finally was able to master three horses on the sulky plow and draw
a straight furrow across the small field south of the barn. After
that, he spent many long days behind that plodding team. It takes
a long time to turn over a field, one twelve inch furrow at a time,
but time was nothing to Albert—he wasn't looking forward to
anything anyway. His proudest moment was when he brought the
plow bottom to Mr. Sexton to show him its state of wear, and to
suggest that it needed to be taken to the blacksmith to be
sharpened.

One part, and only one, on Albert's jacket shows no wear—
the left breast watch pocket. These pockets were standard on men's
work jackets and bib overalls then. The pocket is sewn shut across
the top, but has an opening along the upper part of one side—an
opening large enough to admit a pocket watch. These garments
also featured an extra buttonhole. One end of a watch chain, or
more commonly a braided leather thong, was attached to the
watch, while the other end was secured into this extra buttonhole.
Withdrawing the watch from its hiding place by its leather thong,
holding it up to the light in the palm of the right hand, and
squinting at it with one eye closed, was an almost universal
mannerism of men so equipped. If the watch dial had a protective

cover, which many of them did, snapping open the cover added unspoken volumes to the ceremony.

The watch, snug in its pocket, eventually revealed its presence there by a telltale ring and a slight bulge on the owner's denim breast. But another man who was not a watch owner might sport a similar ring from his snoose box (his tin of Copenhagen Snuff). It took an experienced eye to tell the difference, but a snoose box ring was somewhat larger, and noticeably more distinct, because the snoose box edges were sharp, compared to the rounded contours of a pocket watch. By the time I was a boy, pocket watches were common, and relatively cheap. A boy might hope to get one (a "turnip") for Christmas. But in Albert's day a pocket watch was a mark of some distinction.

Albert's jacket, however, is unsullied by any telltale ring from a pocket watch—or from a snoose box either. Its regular buttonholes are ragged, frayed, or completely torn out, but the extra buttonhole meant for a watch chain is still in pristine condition. Albert was never the owner of a pocket watch. Of course he didn't know how to tell time anyway, except by the sun, but that would not necessarily have been a deterrent. Tales abound of men who, recipients of some windfall, went out and bought watches and chains that they wore proudly, but who could never decipher the mystery of the hands and numbers.

Albert had a last name, but few people knew what it was. He had no social security number, no tax returns, no draft card, and no criminal record, so units of government, whether federal, state, or local, were almost entirely unaware of his existence. Perhaps, in the musty files of a courthouse somewhere, he had (and still has) a birth certificate, but perhaps not. As any genealogy buff can attest, the conscientious recording of births by the government is a relatively new phenomenon.

I feel privileged to be able to give this account of Albert. A warm glow suffuses me as I write. It is little enough, I suppose, a token only, an inadequate effort to celebrate his life on earth. But still—it is probably more than anyone will ever say or write about me after I have been dead for eighty or ninety years.

Trees, By God

Accepted for publication:
North Dakota Quarterly

"Poems," said Joyce Kilmer, "are made by fools like me, but only God can make a tree."

Some would quibble. Disciples of John Calvin might claim that the poems, as well as the tree, were made by God, but many Darwin followers would surely insist that trees are simply the result of eons of natural selection—of evolution, and that God had nothing to do with it.

But what the hell—it's a poem. It doesn't pay to get too literal about poems. Atheist poets routinely invoke God when they need a rhyme.

However it comes about, the making of a tree, and the result of that process, is a wondrous happening for most of us. Thoreau thought trees had souls, and that the individual trees surrounding him at Walden would be his companions in Heaven.

Trees have always been important to mankind. Our distant ancestors lived in trees, relatively safe from predators that stalked the jungle floor below. Without those trees, perhaps there would have been no ancestors for us to spring from. Long before that, the trees of the Paleozoic pumped oxygen into the atmosphere to create what we call air, and the bodies of those same trees furnish coal and oil to sustain us today.

The dense forests that covered central Europe when Julius Caesar went there furnished the wood that built the cities where western culture developed. The English were driven to settle New Brunswick and the other maritime provinces of America when their own tall trees for sailing-ship masts had all been cut down. America was built from wood; in the last century, the magnificent white pine forests on the Minnesota and Wisconsin banks of the St. Croix River furnished profuse quantities of lumber. Much of that lumber is still in use today; new lumber of such quality is virtually unknown. The wanton, wasteful exploitation of those forests stands as a black mark against that chapter of American history.

But all is not lost—trees grow again. The two or three centuries needed to grow a white pine forest giant seem long, but that giant was a seedling once, and even though nearly all of its fellow seedlings perished, vast areas came to be covered with mature white pine. When we think about trees, we need to put aside our penchant for thinking in terms of our own lifetime. Man is not the measure of all things.

By coincidence, as much as by design, trees have become a big factor in my life. In 1961 my wife and I bought a 130-acre place in rural Stillwater, Minnesota, about 25 miles from the laboratory where I worked in St. Paul. The farmer had retired, and had sold off most of his crop land to neighboring farmers. What Ann and I got was a set of farm buildings with the big, old house where I still live, seventy acres of wooded pasture, a shallow lake of about fifty acres that was almost dry at the time, and a few acres of crop land. I rented some additional land, and we farmed part-time for several years. Our operation centered around beef cattle, so the farm buildings and the pasture and crop land were put to good use.

A decade later, things were different. My wife had died, my boys had gone off to college, and my interest in farming had waned. The cattle had been sold, along with most of the farm machinery. Some wet years had filled the lake, and brush was creeping into every open spot in the empty pasture.

More years passed, and the pasture gradually went over to dense woods and undergrowth. Prickly ash, buckthorn, sumac, wild cherry, and hawthorn took over to the extent that it was nearly impossible to get through most areas, even on foot. Wild cherry, and especially Hawthorne, can form formidable obstacles. Hawthorne is a type of wild apple with strong thorns that are about an inch-and-a-quarter-long, and as sharp as Gammer Gurton's needle. It has always seemed incredible to me that nature can produce living things as strong, and as hard, and as sharp as the thorns on a Hawthorne. Harsh experience enables me to give testimony about those thorns. They repeatedly penetrated the six-ply casings on the tractor and Brush Hog tires when I started my brush clearing project. I paid for those tires several times over in repair bills.

My woods are old, and partly populated by mature stands of oak, birch and aspen. These trees are constantly growing, dying and renewing themselves. Storms occasionally topple some of them, or break off large limbs that crash down into the undergrowth. The downed birch and aspen rot away in a few years, but the oak last for decades. A few big oak trees lying tangled together in the brush can effectively preclude access to acres of ground. Napoleon knew—his army engineers impeded the troop movements of opposing armies by felling trees helter-skelter.

By then I had matured a little, along with my trees, and I was thinking more. What should I ultimately do with this land that had then been mine for more than a quarter of a century? I had always vaguely assumed I would eventually try to make some money by subdividing the land into building lots, as most of my neighbors had already done. The lake and the big, mature oak trees made it attractive for that purpose, although road access was something of a problem.

But I had misgivings about such an idea. Land prices in the area were rising rapidly. Some neighbors, who had sold earlier for what seemed then to be a big price, were sorry they had done so. Considered as an investment, holding my land had been profitable. The quickening pace of development in the area suggested that its market value would continue to rise.

Money aside, I found that I had an aversion to the idea of houses on my land, and an even greater aversion to the idea of a public park there. Public parks are fine as major enterprises at the level of Yellowstone or Glacier, and wonderful at the level of city parks in urban areas, but the vainglorious efforts of small township governments to set up park systems degenerate into bureaucratic nightmares that benefit nobody.

So, what would be a good use for this land in the coming years?

The cattle and horses that grazed here for a hundred years, and left a mark in the occasional horseshoe that I dig up in the woods, were not apt to return. This would never be farm country again. It sheltered some wildlife, but the woods had become so dark and deep that even deer were repelled. My family, and neighbors, and friends had once been able to enjoy nature by walking in my woods, but that had become mostly impossible. Parts of the area had always been overgrown, but it had become far worse.

If I wanted to be so selfish as to keep both the bulldozers and the ticket takers from inheriting my land, I needed a constructive idea—some sort of a long-term plan. Was there a way I could determine the future of my land and develop it in such a manner that would give pleasure to me, and to my children and grandchildren, and to my friends and neighbors, and to people in general? And was there a technique by which I could do this and still protect my heirs by retaining the land's value as an investment?

I was, of course, succumbing to one of mankind's universal dreams—the quest for immortality. We want to extend our reach beyond the grave in some way. Most of us hope to do it by having children; Thomas Jefferson did it by writing the Declaration of Independence. I was trying to do it, in a small way, with my land.

And, yes, on further thought, perhaps there was the possibility of such a way. Trees might furnish the centerpiece of such a plan. Trees can, handled properly, constitute a long-term enterprise. If the land had the right kind of trees on it, those trees might furnish a reason for leaving it alone for the next two centuries.

In one sense, for America, this is a great time to plant trees. We deplore the spoiling of nature as shopping malls and highways gobble up farm and forest to create expanses of tarred parking lots, roads, and roofs, but our preoccupation with this aspect of urbanization causes us to ignore a major side effect. Most of the country is actually being depopulated.

Only a few people live in rural Minnesota now. The twin cities of Minneapolis-St. Paul and their suburbs have become huge, and other urban centers like St. Cloud are growing rapidly, but the towns and farms that occupy most of the area of the state have diminished in population. Jackson County, in superb farm country on the Iowa border, is typical. It had a population of 16,805 in 1940. By 1990 that had dwindled to 11,677, and 3,559 of those remaining lived in the city of Jackson, which had actually grown from 2,469 in 1940. Fewer than ten people live on a typical square mile in Jackson County now. Many cities that were once prosperous have suffered substantial reverses, and are characterized by empty stores and houses. Appleton, in west central Minnesota, is such a city. I saw a modern three-bedroom house advertised for sale for $30,000 there.

In South Dakota, this situation is even more extreme. The population of the state as a whole is essentially the same now as it was in 1930, but South Dakota was more than eighty percent rural then. It is fifty percent urban today. Most of the farm homes that once occupied nearly every quarter-section in eastern Dakota have been gone for a long time. A few unkempt trees stand to mark what was once the farmstead grove; the buildings are deserted or gone, the driveway grown over. There are no rural country schools anymore; even the consolidated schools that replaced them are dying. Proposals for combining counties to consolidate services have come before the legislature.

There is something eerie about vast emptiness in a once-busy countryside. Science fiction writers have developed this theme. The plots center around a transportation invention. Its user steps into an isolation booth, punches up a destination, and pushes the "go" button. Instantly, she or he, along with everything else in the booth, is transported to that destination. It makes no difference if the destination is nearby or halfway around the world. After a time, all activity comes to be clustered closely around these stations. The concept of geography, as we know it, becomes lost to ordinary people. No one knows or cares if Station X is in Siberia or in Omaha. The known world consists merely of these stations and their immediate environs. The rest of the earth is, for all practical purposes, off in another dimension, known only to an elite, controlling group who use it for their own nefarious purposes. Rural Minnesota has simply disappeared from the world.

This depopulation of most land areas could leave a lot of room for forests. Even the Midwest, which is intensively farmed, has suitable land. Large parts of northern Minnesota were never better than marginal for agriculture in the first place, and most areas of the state have some land not suitable for large equipment, so there is ample room for trees, and there are few people around to bother them.

96 – At the Oasis

Even in the metropolitan parts of the state, urbanization creates havens for nature. Large areas are zoned for single family dwellings on five-or ten-acre lots. Most homeowners have no way to use this much land, so it stands idle. The result has been a resurgence of wildlife in the urban counties. Bear and beaver are returning to the seven-county metropolitan area. Deer and geese abound again. In the aggregate, thousands of acres that once pastured cattle or produced corn are now given over to box elder, sumac and scrub oak.

So, I reasoned, perhaps my land could become a sort of suburban forest—a spot of wilderness in the shadow of skyscrapers. That would be desirable in itself and it might even start a trend. We have plenty of suitable land in both rural and urban areas. We could have forests if somebody would start them and protect them—why not me? The pines know how to do their part; let's get some in the ground and get going. The longest journey begins with a single step, and all of that.

But there is a big problem. In the long run, money talks, and the incremental annual increase in land value due to timber growth would never pay the taxes and the interest on the real estate investment. There would be financial pressure to subdivide the land into building lots, and that pressure would increase with time. My pines would never be accorded the centuries they would need to mature.

But I thought I saw a possible answer to that problem too. Many houses in my area represent big investments now. It is not uncommon to see an executive or a doctor come out and pump half a million or more into a lot and house. There's a lot of money around.

In spite of their cost, many of these houses of rich men strike me as sterile. Perhaps there are people of such means who might like to buy my place, replace or remodel the house, and keep the land intact–have their own private park, or estate. It would take a lot of work, but many people like to do or manage such work. It would be hard for such a person to find a place better suited to such a project than mine. It has a nice lake, other wetlands, hogbacks and other interesting terrain, and hundreds of big trees.

By the time I had come around to these musings, the land also was, as I have said, a useless, impenetrable jungle. People like to talk about their love of nature in the wild state, but the fact is that woods need to be converted to a comparatively park-like setting before most people will venture into them. I'd have lots of work to do before I could expect a bunch of millionaires to come crawling over each other to help me perpetuate my dream of regal pines towering a hundred and fifty feet above Silver Lake in the year 2200.

If I did clean up my woods, and plant pines in the appropriate places, and take care of them; and if I or my estate executor did then find a rich buyer who shared my dream, would that be enough? Would my giant oaks continue to prosper and drop myriads of acorns to seed new oaks to sustain the progeny of the army of squirrels that chatters there today? Would the Hawthorne continue to erupt into dazzling white to push away the mud of April; would wild grapes festoon whole cedar trees in a drunken orgy of purple each fall? Would sumac still carpet the hillside east of the black spruce swamp in lush, verdant green when June came on a century from now—and would the fall of the year 2100 see that hillside turn into the awe-inspiring red that graced it at sunset yesterday?

And the lake—would the loon still cry over it in the night, would the turtles still dig their eggs into the sandy shore, would the muskrats and the beaver still swim there and build their houses? Would those stark-white egrets and coarse-voiced herons still fish patiently along the swampy shore, and would pairs of stately Canadian Geese still swim proudly with their goslings?

Well—probably not. Not unless I do something more. Rich men are mortal too, and mostly old. When my rich man dies, perhaps thirty years from now, it may be that his heirs in California will not share his enthusiasm for pine-covered hills in Minnesota, not if those hills have come to be worth big bucks by then.

In the legal world, real estate is unique. The ownership of land can be split up in complex ways. I could, perhaps, forestall the rich man's heirs by selling him something less than full title to the property. This might be essential if my plan was to have any hope of long-term success.

98 – At the Oasis

I could, perhaps, first sell covenants to the county, or to my neighbors, specifying that my parcel of land could not be subdivided unless the owners of those covenants agreed. The effectiveness of such agreements fades with time too, but public opinion would eventually favor the preservation of the estate if the surrounding land developed to urban density. No one, not even Ronald Reagan, has tried to sell Central Park in New York City. The first century would be the hard one.

So, I had a plan. A far-fetched one perhaps, but a plan all the same—and the good part came first. I love to work in the woods. Clearing out a brush-clogged draw and converting it into a picturesque hillside with stately oaks overlooking the shore of a pond has become my art. I see myself as akin to the sculptor who chips away all of that extraneous marble to reveal the goddess inside. When I put pine and spruce seedlings into the ground, I do so with an air of excitement about each one. They become my friends, and for years afterward I rush out weekly or monthly to the sites I have cleared and planted so I can check up on each tree.

Trees were vital to my childhood, perhaps because they were so scarce on the Dakota farm homestead my grandparents had wrested from a prairie of waving grass. We had a row of a few scraggly ash along the south side of the dirt driveway that led from our shanty of a house to the dirt road on the section line, and one of those trees was mine. Each of the others was claimed by a brother or a sister.

I went to my tree for solace often, and went there to study its leaves and branches, and to marvel at the designs in its bark and at the strength of its trunk and limbs. It was a safe place, but a place of solitude where a child could observe the world and nature. I was never alone there—not in any negative sense of the word.

In one sense, I suppose, my plan was an excuse—It gave me a reason to work in the woods. I bought a new tractor, and then a larger old one to supplement it, and then an older Caterpillar 955 Traxcavator. I bought saws, and hole diggers, and a tree mover, and a log splitter. I bought grass and weed cutters, and the blacksmith and I became good friends—I designed equipment and he built it for me. This part of the plan would stand or fall based on my own efforts.

The rest of it—the protective covenants and the sale to the rich man—could come later. The IRS rule about step-up in basis upon death favors a strategy where the property is not sold until after I die, anyway. If the plan fails in that phase I probably won't know much about it.

So far, my plan has been working fairly well. Progress has been slower than expected, for several good reasons, but there has been progress. Already, some of my neighbors jokingly refer to my place as McDonald Park, and they go walking there. I've reestablished my boundaries, and built fences to mark them.

Best of all, I'm enjoying the work and its results, and I'm comfortable living here again. I call it a tree farm now. There was a time when I felt out-of-place. It seemed silly to be taking care of a place that wasn't being used for anything.

Now, the long-unused drinking fountains for the cattle and the residual piles of musty hay and manure have been cleaned out of the metal pole barn, and it has been converted into a machine shed/shop for tractors, plows, and other equipment. Another building has been pressed into service for indoor storage of the many cords of firewood that the operation produces as a by-product. I can furnish some employment to teen-aged grandsons during the summer. I have hopes that they will be able to earn college money by selling Christmas trees—the stands will have to be thinned to timber density anyway. My sleepy place has actually acquired a certain air of bustle at times.

If Nature has been, for me, the provider of beauty, variety, and wonder, she has also been a stern adversary. At one point, I started building a field road along the lake shore, a distance of about three quarters of a mile. For centuries, that shore has been the scene of a battle between forest and lake. A series of dry years causes the lake to recede, leaving behind a mud flat dotted with abandoned muskrat houses. In a flash, the forest moves forward. Cocklebur and fast-growing aspen and box elder trees claim the land. After a decade or two the strongest trees have shot toward the sky, and trunks a foot in diameter stand where fish swam and coot cavorted in their lunatic mien.

But wet years return, and the lake rises again, inundating those wooded areas. The trees, large and small, die. Their rotting skeletons point skyward from the swamp for a few years, but they eventually crash down into it and lie there like an underwater abattoir. Given time, they rot away or sink into the mud.

It was into this battle that I had decided to inject myself when I started my road around the lake. I needed a better road to get equipment back to places where I was clearing or planting, but my idea of having it along the shore was also prompted by another consideration.

I wanted to bring order to this chaos. If I could establish a road along the high-water line I could doze the debris out into the water when it receded, and could keep those areas free of brush and trees thereafter. The road would also furnish a good base for work on the forest side, and would double as a hiking trail with good access to both the lake and the woods.

My "road" was more of a trail, but it was adequate for tractors and hikers. Building it took a lot of work and expense, but the results were pleasing. When I finished, it was doing what it was designed to do. The water was still quite high, and I was waiting for it to recede so I could do more work on the lake side of the road. I envisioned meadow-like areas there during periods of low water–possibly I could plant some corn there to feed the wildlife.

Then one year the normally dry month of August brought unprecedented rainfall. Instead of receding, the lake rose further. Soon part, then all, of my road disappeared beneath the waves. The oldest settler had no recollection of that lake ever being so high. Wet summers continued, and my road wasn't seen for years. I was driven to move it to higher ground, and to construct grades with culverts or bridges where swampy areas emptied into the lake.

Nature has played me other tricks too. At one point a tornado roared through my woods, filling them with debris from houses and barns it blew down, and ripping out dozens of huge oaks. A forest ranger examined the aftermath, and told me that many of the downed oaks were good enough and big enough for lumber, but capitalizing on that potential turns out to be a difficult enterprise too. Many of the trees are down on steep hillsides or hung up in other trees, and they weigh tons.

Such setbacks are discouraging, but I'm working smarter now, and the weather has changed again, so I still have confidence in my original goal.

I started with two thousand seedlings, and the largest of these are now at least fifteen feet tall. Subsequent plantings are doing well too. Some were put in open ground with a tree-planting machine, but others were set in individual auger holes spotted between oak stumps. Some areas were so thick with brush that I doubt if any human foot had been set there in fifty years. The soil below was fertile, and the roots remained in place, so the brush and weeds and grass are still fighting to reclaim their home from my invading pines. Some of the spruce and pines will need my protection for a few years yet, but eventually they will be large enough to shade the ground and gain final victory.

On a vastly larger scale, this battle between grass and trees, and between different species of trees, was waged across the Midwest without man's intervention for millennia. Each can protect itself from the others, once it gains ascendancy. Trees dominated the whole eastern half of what was to become the United States, but eventually, in Minnesota, "the prairie stopped the pine." Rainfall and soil conditions were the ultimate arbiters.

Actually, it would be more accurate to say the prairie stopped the oak. The "Pineries" lay almost exclusively east of the Mississippi River. They were dominated by Pinus Strobus, the five-needled white pine that grew for centuries and came to be five feet in diameter and two hundred feet tall. West of the river and extending to and beyond the Minnesota River, lay the "Big Woods," a terminal forest of hardwoods dominated by huge, imperial oaks. Both are gone now—lumbermen took the pine, and the oaks were simply cut and burned to clear the land.

Working in the woods is a humbling experience. I try to be very careful not to destroy anything unless it is absolutely necessary, but sometimes the Brush Hog has to mangle and shred a beautiful oak sapling to get through. Also, sometimes, the dead oak that I fell crashes down and crushes a lovely young maple tree that had prospered in its small niche for twenty years, and might have gone on to become an imposing Grande Dame of the forest. When this happens, I feel as if I have just killed another soldier in battle, and I don't even know which side either of us was on.

102 – At the Oasis

Even the cocklebur is a magnificent plant, with its blue fuzz blossoms and a structure tough as whang leather. Its great rough leaves are a very model of the power of photosynthesis. Observed impartially, the cocklebur plant is a most imposing entity. It fairly leaps from the ground in the spring, even while the snow lingers, and it subsides in the fall only after a very severe freeze. In between times, it rises up into a virtual tree, shouldering aside lesser plants and branching out until it stands alone to challenge all comers. It is hard to imagine a tougher specimen—hack it down and it springs forth anew from whatever you leave. If there are miracles on this earth, then surely, the cocklebur is one of them. If there were only a few, they would be held sacred by some major religion. It seems almost criminal to try to destroy such a glorious product of nature.

But down they go, and down they must go if this area is to be anything but an impenetrable jungle in my lifetime, or that of my children. As the perpetrator of this carnage, I console myself with the knowledge that nature herself is far more ruthless in these matters than I am.

Joyce Kilmer may be right, but God makes millions of trees where only a few can grow. In my woods it's up to God the Second—me—to decide who lives and who dies, and I'm awed by the responsibility. I think that I'm doing the right thing, but then I look back at the trail of shredded organic matter behind me and reflect that it represents what was, moments earlier, thousands of lives. I sometimes cringe then, and an insistent voice makes itself heard, not above, but within, the roar of the tractor motor. Tyrant—it whispers. Tyrant!

Those who wield power bear a heavy burden, but we persevere in the knowledge that chaos will conquer if we falter, and chaos makes the world worse, not better. Once I get this wilderness under control, my farm will be wonderful. The pines will tower to the heavens, and take care of themselves. Oaks and maples will spread leafy canopies over the hills, fish and frogs and muskrats will thrive in the lake, and deer will graze in open meadows along the shore. Joyce Kilmer would surely approve. I could leave no better gift to posterity.

The Future

Tracey was just bringing LaVerne his breakfast of eggs and white toast as I slid onto the stool beside him. His first cup of coffee was almost empty, so she filled that up too, and put another cupful in front of me.

"Well, how's it going today?" he inquired as he dug into his pocket for special little shakers of seasoning forced upon him by the doctor in lieu of the salt and pepper offered by the Oasis Café. Verne had a lot of health problems. His stays at the Oasis were shorter than they used to be because he soon had to get back out to his truck and the oxygen bottles mounted there in the cab.

"Can't complain," I answered. "Nobody would listen anyway. How's farming?"

"Good. The kid got done planting corn yesterday. Hosed the planter down and got it back in the shed." The corn planter had been an occasional topic of conversation all winter. It was new—second hand new—and a monster. Just figuring out all of the mechanics and hydraulics to unfold it into its field configuration had been a day's job—for "the kid" (Donny), that is, not for Verne. Verne's health no longer permitted him such activity.

"How much did he end up putting in?" I asked.

"I don't know exactly. Something over seven hundred acres. I know they had the damn thing over in Minnesota twice."

I whistled softly. Seven hundred acres of corn in the ground probably represents an investment approaching a hundred thousand dollars. Donny is a hard charger who hunts up farm land to rent for miles around. The Andersons live in Wisconsin, just across the St. Croix River from Stillwater, Minnesota, where we were talking at the Oasis Café. Verne had lived on that farm all of his life, and had attended elementary school in Stillwater in the

104 – At the Oasis

1930s, walking across the interstate bridge every morning and evening, so he had a sort of a fatherly interest in that bridge.

"Herding that rig across the lift bridge and through the narrow streets of Stillwater must have been awesome," I commented. "Did they have any trouble?"

"Not much. They always went at five-thirty in the morning. There's no boats, so the lift is always down, and the road traffic is pretty light."

"Well, better him than me—I'm glad I don't have to do it. My concept of farming runs more to a team of horses on a single row cultivator."

Verne laughed. "Me too, really. I can't even keep track of what the hell he's doing half of the time. My dad would turn over in his grave if he could see what farming is like now."

I think of my father too, and of my grandfather who died in 1893, both lifetime farmers, and I imagine what it would be like for them to see the farms of today—or those of tomorrow. Who even knows what the farms of tomorrow will be like? Who knows what anything will be like, for that matter? The farms are not the only things that have changed.

Verne and I often talk of the future and of the past, as do many others. Obviously, none of us will ever know if our speculations end up close to the mark or ridiculously far from it. Even our best established and most cherished institutions often have to give way before new and relentless economic and social realities—sometimes by gradual evolution, sometimes by drastic, revolutionary, changes that seem to arise almost overnight. We can never know what will happen, but I think we do influence it by talking about it. It is as though, from these innumerable and diverse discussions, something akin to consensus eventually arises.

An *Essay on the Origin of Schatzheim*

The accuracy of hindsight is legendary, so I choose here to step into the future and look back at a period that is actually still ahead of us. Such an approach may be questionable, but I apply it to an area where nothing else has worked very well anyway.

I refer to our many attempts to solve the problems that plague the children of the inner city and, to a lesser extent, some children everywhere. On their behalf I have, in another writing, invented a place, a social institution called Schatzheim, and peopled it partly with an imaginary family I call the Oelkers. This essay describes Schatzheim and looks back upon its operation from some unspecified vantage point a few decades into the future.

So what is this Schatzheim, this place where the Oelkers live, this place that Josh and Julie call home?

Schatzheim is a family orphanage.

What is a *family orphanage*?

Family orphanages were born as a result of a crisis in America. As the 21st century opened, America was awash in unprecedented affluence—big cars, huge houses, and Caribbean cruises were the order of the day. But a large element of American society did not share this affluence, and that element consisted largely of children—the children of the inner city who often subsisted in drug-crazed, brutal poverty. Abused, starved, and beaten, deprived of any significant education, these lost souls grew up to become the predatory, soulless abusers of the next generation, or their feckless pawns, and so the cycle went, on and on, generation after generation. The cost was incalculable.

The conventional political wisdom of that day talked of solutions in terms of fault, and much of the fault was laid at the door of the parents. The solution, according to this school of thought, was to insist that the parents who brought these children into the world take hold and fulfill their responsibility. Never mind that the concept of parents, in the plural, was almost unknown in that society, and never mind that most of these parents had never been able to take care of themselves, much less someone else. Pressure on these uneducated, battered, single mothers would somehow solve problems that congress, with its billions, could only debate.

As the situation worsened, a cry arose to the effect that we should break this cycle by taking the children away from these parents if necessary. One might argue about fault, the proponents said, but one could not reasonably suggest that the children were at fault. These children deserved to grow up in a safe place and be educated so that they could eventually take a place as productive members of our society. Social workers were urged to move more rapidly towards a legal remedy—*Termination of Parental Rights* or TPR. It was time to forego any obsessive interest in the rights of the parents, and to give first consideration to the best interests of the child.

By this theory, in its most extreme form, the question of whether or not the parent was at fault became irrelevant. If a child was not being properly cared for, then the State should step in. The effect, on the child, of a parent who could not function was indistinguishable from that of a parent who would not function. Unfair to some parents? Perhaps, they said, but the court's first responsibility is to the child, not the parent.

Such Orwellian measures are viewed with great distrust in America, even in the presence of crisis, and for many excellent reasons. Who would raise such a mass of court-made orphans, and how? What would it cost, and what kind of citizens would it produce? And besides, many of these single mothers, and some single fathers and couples too, are failing as parents only because they are overwhelmed by their surroundings and lack the will and strength to escape. In a different environment they could love, and be loved by, their children, and contribute enormously in many ways to their upbringing.

From this crisis, and this debate about it, a new social institution finally emerged. It came to be called the family orphanage—a place where children who needed a home could go, with or without their parents. There were growing pains as the institution matured, and it developed somewhat differently in different cities, but Schatzheim is a fairly good example of the modern family orphanage.

Schatzheim is a somewhat authoritarian place; adults who live there have to follow the rules, and are subject to being monitored in that respect, and to being expelled for violations. Privacy is limited, but it is a safe place where children can live and grow.

An adult has to apply in order to be able to live at Schatzheim; no adult can be forced to live there. When a court decides that children are not being adequately cared for and orders Schatzheim to take custody of them, many adult parents, and some grandparents, apply in order to be able to stay with their children. Not all adults who apply are accepted. Some parents apply for admission to Schatzheim on behalf of themselves and their children, a process akin to voluntary commitment. Often, these are single mothers or mothers in an abusive relationship. The term "parent" here is used in a broad sense to include any adult who has legal custody.

When adult parents are admitted to Schatzheim along with their children, legal custody of the children is shared between Schatzheim and the parents. Any adult can leave at any time, but children can only be removed with court approval. An adult parent who leaves his or her children there usually loses custody of them, and Schatzheim then takes full custody.

Minor children can become residents of Schatzheim only by court order. The order, which gives certain authority over the child to the institution, may arise upon a social worker's initiative, such as a petition to terminate parental rights, or it may arise from a petition by a parent.

Other adults are only admitted to Schatzheim for the benefit of the children. Some are closely associated with a resident family or resident children (grandparents, for example), while a few others are public-spirited individuals (often professionals) who volunteer to live and work at Schatzheim.

Schatzheim is a city within a city—a "walled" city with strictly controlled access through guarded gates. It has very little automobile traffic. Residents are allowed to have cars, but few can afford them, and many residents seldom go outside the walls anyway. Public transportation is readily available outside the gates; in fact these areas have become hubs for all kinds of public transport. There are parking lots and ramps immediately inside the gates, and most vehicles go no further than that. Schatzheim is well served with internal public transport, much of it in the form of automatic trains, moving sidewalks, and elevators. This approach works well because the city is compact and well engineered.

Schatzheim is also, of course, a subsidized city. Much of its budget comes from the public money that formerly went to welfare payments and foster care. A significant part does come, however, from rent paid by residents. Charity from foundations and private citizens is also a factor.

About half of the children at Schatzheim now have one or more parents there with them. This proportion has steadily increased. Many of the children without parents are housed with a Schatzheim family in a sort of a foster care status. Others live in a group home (orphanage) environment patterned after places like Boy's Town in Nebraska.

Schatzheim is a city that stresses service. Day care, for example, is available as part of their rent to all residents and operates around the clock, 365 days a year. Children are welcome there. A parent whose children spend all of their time at the day care center will eventually face some sharp questions from the management, but the children are welcomed with open arms anytime they come and for as long as they stay. They always have a home there. For infants without families, it is their only home. Other children live in a group home or with families, but they are always welcome at the day care center, which includes a recreation center and a library. Schatzheim children grow up regarding the day care center as a natural, everyday, part of their lives. It is an animated place that supervises a busy recreational program and other diverse activities.

Other services include the public cafeteria or dining hall, where most people eat, the public laundries, and a movie theater. These communal arrangements are favored partly to simplify the living quarters, but they are also meant to serve a sociological purpose. Many residents come from backgrounds where they have developed only limited social skills, as well as limited housekeeping and homemaking skills. The plan is to develop an environment that will maximize social interaction outside the home, while also furnishing a simple home environment that can be easily managed and supervised. One of Schatzheim's aims is to teach independent living skills. Residents are encouraged to prepare for the day when they can leave if they wish to. Some parents do eventually regain full custody of their children and leave through a transitional program.

Other public facilities within the city include churches, entertainment centers, and stores and shops. Grocery stores and restaurants are rare because dining hall meals are included as part of the rent and the apartments lack kitchens, but entrepreneurship is encouraged, and some residents operate shops, such as beauty shops or hobby shops.

All able-bodied adults and teenagers work and pay rent. Many work at outside jobs, but many others are employed within the city, and some do both. Almost all of the people who work within Schatzheim are residents. The day care program and the dining hall are major employers, both of adults and of part-time teen-agers. The security department, the administration and records department, and a city maintenance operation also employ a substantial number of the residents.

Schatzheim does not have its own school system—the children attend public school. There has been debate about this, and some similar institutions in other cities have set up their own school systems. The prevailing opinion here is that, although the public school environment is not as safe as the one at Schatzheim, it is quite safe or can be made so. The children will eventually be going out into the world, and public school is a good way to start to adapt them to that world.

The city aims to provide a safe environment for its residents by excluding illegal drugs, abusive visitors, and other threats to their well-being. The gate into Schatzheim has been likened to the sally port of a prison, with armed guards, remotely operated steel gates, and TV surveillance cameras. The guards have had to repel gate crashers on a number of occasions over the years, and there have been two gun battles there, but nothing recently. The reputation of the Schatzheim gate as a place ready and able to defend its turf against all comers has spread. Any visitor may be detained and searched as a condition of admittance or while in the city, or may be refused admittance for past conduct, unless a court orders otherwise. Adult residents who violate the rules are subject to summary ejection from Schatzheim, as well as to prosecution for any unlawful acts. Juvenile violators may be subjected to additional controls and/or referred to outside authorities.

Although their actions are subject to review by an elected Council of Residents as well as by an outside administrative agency and by the court, the authorities at Schatzheim are given wide discretion in matters of security. Given reasonable cause, for example, they are free to use listening devices or surveillance cameras within living quarters or anywhere else in the city. Residents are encouraged to report illegal activity, and may do so anonymously.

Despite these stringent security rules, Schatzheim is largely self-governing. Their elected Council of Residents is officially only an advisory body, but except in budgetary matters, the council's decisions are seldom overturned. A county commissioner sits on the council as an ex-officio member. Most workers in the Safety and Security Dept. are also residents, so the security guards have close ties to the community. A special rule limits tenure in Security to five years. The purpose of the rule is to avoid any danger that an abusive security "dynasty" might develop. Wary watchdog civil rights organizations outside Schatzheim also monitor this aspect of the operation closely.

The Schatzheim name arose as a corruption of German words. "Schatz," can be taken in the sense of "sweetheart," and its diminutive, "schatzi'" is often applied as a term of endearment to young children, while "heim" is offered in the sense of "home." Before the name caught on some people were in the habit of referring to the institution as "The Swiss Family Orphanage," in a whimsical sonogram reference to an old book, The Swiss Family Robinson.

The family orphanage concept drew a storm of protest when it was first presented. It was denounced variously as communist, dictatorial, patronizing, racist, un-American, ungodly, fascist, big brother, crack pot, do-gooder, quixotic, spendthrift criminal nonsense; but the inner city problems of slums, drugs, crime, loss of social structure, and legions of lost children finally forced action anyway. Since then, in the eyes of its proponents, Schatzheim has been a resounding success, and the concept has been adopted in many urban areas.

Proponents point to thousands of children growing up safe, secure, and happy, and to children now emerging as well-educated productive adults, ready to take a responsible role in the outside world. Proponents have also silenced many of their erstwhile critics by pointing out that even the direct dollar costs of welfare are down—well below their previous levels. Schatzheim has not only cut the social cost immeasurably, it has also reduced the dollar cost significantly, they crow.

These undoubted successes have driven many critics from the field, but a vehement hard core of detractors remains. "These Schatzheim children may appear to be educated and well adjusted," they say, "but they have been produced by a paternalistic society that values security over freedom. Such a choice goes against everything we stand for. Our founding fathers risked everything for freedom, and succeeding generations have overwhelmingly endorsed that choice. Schatzheim children will become adults who are ready-made for slavery—high class slavery, perhaps, but slavery all the same. And we do them no favor because slaves are never happy. Such children deserve our pity, not our praise. If they are well-educated it only makes matters worse. They may succeed to high places and inculcate our society with their false values. Schatzheim children are a menace to America! We must waste no time in doing away with this ungodly system."

Proponents scoff at such overblown rhetoric. "Security has always been an important consideration," they say. "Look back at what these children would have become under the old system. Anyway, compared to the population at large, only a small, vulnerable group is afforded the special security of Schatzheim. They pose no threat to America; we hope that one of them becomes president some day."

Perhaps one way to judge the merit of Schatzheim is to look at some case histories. A few representative ones are presented below:

Case #1: JB had never wanted to live at Schatzheim. She was, figuratively speaking, dragged there, kicking and screaming. It is true that no adult can be forced to live at Schatzheim against her will, but the judge, a woman with iron-gray hair and a steely gaze, made JB an offer she could not refuse. The children were going to Schatzheim, the judge said. JB could either volunteer to live at Schatzheim with them, or she could go her own way, lose the children altogether, and perhaps also face charges of criminal child neglect. JB opted for Schatzheim, and even crawled and licked some boots when Schatzheim expressed doubt about whether they wanted her or would even accept her.

Licking those boots was hard for JB. She prided herself on a fierce independence, which seemed to apply to everybody except to a series of crumb bum boy friends who had beat her around for years and left her with two children—a five-year-old boy and a two-year-old girl, both of uncertain parentage. Twenty-three now, she had run away from a suburban home in another state as a rebellious teen-ager, and had taken up life on the streets here.

Although part of the drug scene, she had not, herself, been a significant user. She had held a series of jobs, showed promise on some of them, but always eventually got into some kind of a fracas over her extreme independence, and stormed off. At home she was hopeless; her house was always a pigpen, and she was an equal mess, except when she went out somewhere. She was full of blame for the landlord, the neighbors, the social workers, her parents, or anyone else who came to mind. She moved from one apartment to another, followed by a host of bill collectors and the forlorn detritus of the city. Both children were yet to be toilet trained, and the family had a welfare department case number of four years standing.

The boy friend was in his thirties, and had a criminal record that included incarceration for assault. He was, according to the boy, "just plain mean." Despite the social worker's warning, JB had left him alone with the children. He was drinking, the children were sick, and he had thrown the little girl against a wall because she wouldn't stop crying. Later, when he was passed out on the bed, the boy called 911 to say that his little sister was lying on the floor, bleeding from the mouth. An arrest followed. The little girl recovered in the hospital, and joined her brother in temporary foster care. Soon after that, JB found herself standing before the judge with the iron-gray hair.

JB was delighted to have her children back with her when they moved into Schatzheim. She had felt real shame when she saw her daughter in the hospital, and the doctor warned her that the little girl might die. She steeled herself to turn her back on the boyfriend when they hauled him off to a long prison sentence. She thought of her childhood home, and, for the first time, conceded to herself that the mess her life was in might be largely her own fault and that she had failed her children. She had heard many horror stories about foster care, but the two months her children had been there seemed to have been good for them. They were energetic, their color was better, and the boy was completely toilet trained, and proud of it. She, herself, had a job and was resolved that this time she would shut her big mouth and keep it shut.

The worker who welcomed them and showed them around Schatzheim was very detailed and specific about the rules. She and her supervisor had studied JB's case thoroughly, and they were quite concerned. JB would have to drastically remake herself to fit in here, and the rules were clear. Schatzheim would give no quarter, and infractions could, would if continued, lead to expulsion. She was, essentially, on probation.

J.B's spleen nearly erupted during this meeting, but, for almost the first time in her life, she kept her tongue and her demeanor under control. "I can play their game," she thought. "It must be just a game. No place on earth could possibly be as regimented as this sounds to hear them tell it. It'll be like an initiation. After a few days or weeks, the bulk of it'll be over and we'll be able to settle in here. Maybe it won't be so bad. It is nice and clean and organized, and that day care center looks really good for the kids while I'm at work, or if I want to go out somewhere."

She managed to meet the minimum requirements during the first month, although barely. They complained about the housekeeping in her apartment after only a week, and harassed her with daily inspections after that until she finally buckled down and started to take care of it regularly. After the kids missed several meals at the dining hall, and they found junk food in her apartment, they called her before the nutrition board for a discussion. And when she failed several times to show up at the scheduled time to pick up the kids from day care (she had stopped for a drink after work) they asked for an explanation. By then, she had talked to others and seen enough to know that there would be no let up. She would learn to do it their way, or else.

By the time the second month was over she was feeling very depressed. It seemed to her that the kids were growing away from her. They had always been totally dependent on her— hollow-eyed, listless, pitiful, craving the slightest attention that she might bestow upon them. Now they were bright-eyed and energetic, had friends and activities, and didn't seem to notice much whether she was even there or not. It was a new experience for her. She found herself trying to win their favor, and hated herself for it. She had no friends at Schatzheim, was sex starved, and longed for the old days.

One day after work she ran into a guy who had once been the boy friend of a friend of hers. He invited her to a party. She went, had a wonderful time, stayed with him all night, and went directly from his bed to her job in the morning. Later that afternoon, when she got off work she returned to Schatzheim, slipped her card into the slot, and walked through the turnstile as usual. But this time her card did not come back on the other side. Instead, a bell rang and a guard stepped out and ushered her into a tiny interview room where she cooled her heels for the next hour, growing angrier and more defiant by the minute.

When an interviewer finally came in and started asking questions, she blew up. It felt good to be telling someone off—like old times—and she let herself go completely, ranting and raving and storming around the room as she had always done as a teen-ager in her parents home.

He let her go for about five minutes, then pointed to the video recorder that was taking it all in, and handed her two pieces of paper, standard forms. The first was a TPR Petition asking the court to terminate her parental rights, and a temporary order, giving Schatzheim temporary full custody of her children. The second paper was a summons ordering her to appear in court the next week to show cause why the temporary order should not be made permanent. She could stay in her apartment until the court date, but would not be allowed any contact with the children.

JB stormed out of the interview room, went to her apartment, and started throwing things and kicking holes in the walls. It was a bad idea; she should have remembered that there were TV monitors in the apartments. Two armed guards came through the door almost immediately, put her in handcuffs, and took her to a holding cell where they left her alone for two hours so she could cool off. Then they escorted her back to the apartment, gave her twenty minutes to pack what she could carry, and evicted her from the city.

She failed to appear for the court hearing the following week, and apparently never saw Schatzheim, or her children, again.

Case #2: MR came to Schatzheim by a different route. The oldest child of four, she had always been seen as plain and not overly bright. Always a home body, she had lived with her parents until they both died when she was thirty. By then, all of her siblings were gone from the home, although the youngest, a girl of eighteen, still lived in the city and came around from time to time, usually to ask her parents for money, which they mostly had none of. Her brothers, in their twenties then, had left town and the family seldom even heard of them.

In contrast to her younger sister, MR had never shown any great interest in boys or men. She worked at a menial job in a cafeteria, and pooled her pay with the meager resources of her parents to help pay the rent and buy the groceries. In their own way, the three of them were quite comfortable and happy.

After the death of her parents, MR moved. The apartment was too large for her. She could not afford the rent, and she felt uncomfortable there anyway—unsettled. It was as if she was always waiting for them to come home. Her new home was called a "studio apartment"—one room plus a tiny kitchenette, a bathroom, and a closet. The bed was a "Murphy" that pulled down from a recess in the wall; its mattress was hard, but MR was a healthy, muscular girl, and she slept fine there. She brought along a few favorite pieces of furniture, pictures, curios, and kitchen equipment from the old place, and was quite proud of her new digs.

The trouble, and the joy, started after she had been there for two years. Her younger sister, who she had seldom seen since the death of their parents, started bringing her two-year-old boy around for MR to baby sit. Sis never left a telephone number, and MR didn't have a telephone or any need of one anyway. Sis was always vague about where she and the boy lived or who the father was, but she came equipped with toys, books to read, and instructions about toilet training and food—she had always been a bossy thing anyway.

The boy was trouble enough, keeping him corralled, out of stuff, fixing him a place to sleep, reading to him, getting him to the toilet—it was endless, but this was part of the joy. He was learning to walk and talk, and MR became devoted to the effort, clearing spaces, repeating words, holding him on her lap while she read to him and he fell asleep there, putting him down for his nap or for the night. He soon knew her name, and rushed to hug her when they came. MR had never been loved before, and the experience was overwhelming.

The real trouble was with the sister, and her irresponsible way of not coming back to pick up her son when she was supposed to. MR had her job, and it had always been the center of her life. She was never, never, late for work, nor did she ever allow anything to distract her from her duties when she was on the job. In a better organization, her past performance would have earned her accolades by now. But the management was one of the most transient parts of the organization where she worked, and most of her immediate bosses didn't know whether she had been there for ten years or ten weeks. There were employee records that could be consulted, but they seldom were. MR simply assumed, and she was partly right, that her job hung by a thread, subject to good performance, and that each day was a new chapter.

So, eventually, a time came when she had the boy and it was time for her to go to work, but her sister had not appeared. This situation posed, for MR, perhaps the greatest crisis of her life. She rushed about in consternation and finally, late already, took the boy with her and tried to explain her problem to an unsympathetic supervisor. He sent her back home without pay, and suggested that she should call a social worker. He even had a telephone number for her to call, because situations like this were distressingly common with many of the feckless employees he was called upon to supervise. "And get yourself a damned telephone," he fairly snarled at her as she departed.

This double blow to her meager budget threw her into such turmoil that she didn't call the number even after the phone was in. Her sister had apologized, something MR had never seen before in their lifetime together, and the crisis seemed to recede. She was quite nervous about the idea of a social worker anyway, and the telephone added a new interest to her life.

But then it happened again—and again, and again, sometimes for days on end. The second time she did call the number her former supervisor had given her (he was gone by then), and found out that it wasn't actually the welfare department, but was something called "Employee Relations" at a higher level in the corporation that owned the cafeteria where she worked. It turned out that they did have an "Emergency Day Care Facility" for employees, and she could take the boy there. She had to leave a half hour early, and the cost was substantial, but she fell into the habit of doing it that way.

Over a period of months, her sister's absences became more prolonged, and MR became the defacto custodian of the boy. They were wonderful together, but the strain this arrangement put on her budget was intolerable. She was behind with her day care payment, behind with her rent, behind with everything. The landlord was threatening to evict her and her employer was threatening to hold up her little paycheck. Then she came home from work one day and found a note on her door. It was from her sister, who said that she had to go to California, and wasn't sure when she would be able to come back. A shopping bag with a toy for the boy lay on the doorsill.

She went to the telephone again, called the Employee Relations Department, and tried to explain about her problem with the day care bill. This time her call was transferred to an in-house social worker. MR was able to lay out her situation in some detail while the worker perused the employee history which she had called up on the screen before her. "I think you should talk with the people at Schatzheim," the worker finally said. "I'll set up an interview if that's O.K."

"What is Schatzheim?" said MR.

A visit to Schatzheim followed, and MR, buried in her dilemmas, saw it as a piece of Heaven on earth. Days later, they were in court for a perfunctory appearance in which MR and Schatzheim were given temporary joint custody of the boy. The corporation forgave the day care debt in the form of a deductible gift to Schatzheim, and a schedule of payments was worked out for MR to settle up with her landlord. Soon after that, MR and the boy became Schatzheim residents.

In this case, nothing could have been better. MR returned to her exemplary performance as an employee, and the peace of mind it brought her. The boy thrived at Day Care when she was away, gaining skills and friends. When she was home, which was all of the time she wasn't at work, they prospered in their comparatively roomy Schatzheim apartment, at the dining hall, and around the city. For almost the first time in her life, MR began to cultivate a circle of friends with common interests, and she started to find ways to help other children, especially those who were in the group homes.

They are still there. The boy is in elementary school now, and doing well. MR has left her job at the cafeteria to become a Schatzheim employee. It appears likely that they will spend their lives there until the boy graduates and goes out into the world, and that MR will continue there even after that.

Case #3: G&A G have three children. The youngest, a boy, T, has a severe physical handicap. GG has a steady job; he works as a clerk at a bank. AG also had a job in the early years of the marriage before T was born, but taking care of a handicapped son and his two older sisters proved to be a full time job for her, and she was not able to work outside of the home after that.

Despite his handicap, T was a lovable child, and his family closed about him in an insular way. Until the girls became old enough to start school the family had few contacts outside the home except for GG's job. T made little progress, perhaps because everybody else was always so anxious to do things for him.

But as T was turning four, his two sisters were in the second and third grades, and the world was changing for their family. The girls saw other handicapped kids who had been mainstreamed into classrooms, and talked with them and with their counselors about their brother. The stories came home and led to conversations between the counselors and the girls' mother, and eventually to evaluations for T and a gradual immersion in the world of special education and training for the handicapped. T deserved an opportunity to be all that he could be, and his family was determined to give him that chance.

But they were already somewhat strapped financially, living from one paycheck to the next. There was help available, public and private assistance for special education, but there were no end of new problems. He had to be here, and he had to be there, he had to have this, and he had to have that. The house was unsuitable, he needed wheelchair access to the special bus, an on and on. The family was in frenzy, desperate to keep up because the programs were doing wonders for T.

Finally, someone suggested that they consider Schatzheim, and they looked into it. The rent there would be substantial for them, but it would free them up so that both parents could work. Schatzheim had good facilities for handicapped kids, and excellent connections with outside agencies.

Voluntarily moving into a place with so many rules and restrictions on freedom might be daunting for some families, but they talked about it and decided that it wouldn't really bother them. The little girls found the idea of going to a public dining hall for meals as a family to be appealing. As to the future, there were no guarantees, but Schatzheim and the court were generally cooperative when a family decided that they wanted to leave Schatzheim if the family could show that they had a practical plan for living on the outside and it appeared the children would be safe there.

So, if things got better, and they wanted to, they could probably leave Schatzheim at some time in the future. If things didn't get better, or until they did, it seemed to them that this might be the place for them. Finally, after a couple of weeks of soul searching, they decided to go for it, and petitioned the court to be admitted to Schatzheim.

That was several years ago, and they are still there. T is thriving, and the family has emerged from its former isolation. They have few luxuries, but they are comfortable, and are actually saving money. G&AG and their family are seen by Schatzheim, and by themselves, as a living example of the good that can come from such an institution.

Case #4: For her various social workers, AR was one of the most frustrating cases they had ever been called upon to deal with. Fiercely independent, AR seemed to crave conflict. She grew up in Detroit in a comfortable, middle-class home, and her main interest in life seemed to be to find ways in which she could aggravate her mother. She fought with everybody but she took a positive glee in anything she could do to create anguish for her mother. She had only dim memories of her father, who had died when she was little.

Even at age thirty, after four kids of her own, after an abortion at age fifteen, and with a concussion from being kicked in the head by her lately acquired husband, during interviews she would revert to the mannerisms of a bratty thirteen-year-old and smirk about the way she could "jerk her mother around." It was a favorite phrase for AR; she also "jerked that psychiatrist around" when, at fifteen, she was sent to an all-girl Catholic school because she had been making a practice of climbing over a fence to meet a "gang banger" who was seventeen. She did finish high school though, after getting kicked out twice for fighting, and bore her first live baby a few weeks later. After another twenty months of hanging around the house and harassing her mother to death, she had another baby. This finally put mom over the wall, and she kicked AR out of the house.

For the next seven years she continued to kick around Detroit, moving in and out of the Milos Kryszka housing project in Hamtramac, living with various relatives, or in motels. She worked as a waitress most of the time, lost at least two jobs for fighting, and had two more babies. She was also homeless for several months, during which time her children stayed (where else) with her mother. She was in trouble of one kind or another most of the time, and a legend among the social workers and courts of Detroit.

But AR had another side too. A self-professed "strong woman," she was a demon for work, amazingly resourceful, and would do anything for her kids—anything except control her temper and behave herself, that is. She often worked at more than one job, and many of her employers swore by her—for a while. One acquaintance from the West likened her to a coyote—ruthless, resourceful, industrious, and sex crazy.

Eventually, an argument erupted in which she stabbed another woman. The wound was superficial, and the woman stabbed did not press charges—in fact, she skipped out of town. Even so, AR was charged, and brought before a judge who considered what he had, and then made AR an offer she couldn't refuse—leave town or go to jail.

So she moved to our city, met this guy, and got married. He wasn't exactly a prize either, although he had a job and they did fairly well for a couple of years. They had a good apartment and two cars (with big payments due each month), and the kids were in school. It didn't last though, he kept getting heavier into drugs, this caused financial problems, she started working two jobs and was gone all of the time, he quit work entirely, hung around home, and became abusive toward the neighbors. The landlord finally sent an eviction notice, they fought about that, and he kicked her in the head in front of her kids. She went to the hospital, he went to jail, and the kids went to emergency foster care.

The social worker assigned to the case went to Detroit, came back with a complete account of AR's tumultuous life there, decided that enough was enough, and filed a petition for termination of parental rights.

"These kids belong in Schatzheim," she said. "And preferably without that mother of theirs."

Schatzheim agreed, and refused to accept AR as a resident. She stormed out of a first interview, returned contrite a week later, actually begged later, and even got her mother to come from Detroit to plead her case, but Schatzheim was adamant. She would be bad for both her children and for Schatzheim, they said.

And so it would have ended, except for the fact that the children were very upset by the prospect of not ever being able to see their mother again. Faced with this, and with some political pressure, Schatzheim did finally relent to the extent of allowing visitation for AR, and for her mother. In AR's case the grant came with a stern warning that her right of visitation would be withdrawn if she started any trouble or failed to abide by the rules when she came to Schatzheim to visit.

So the future of this case is still in doubt. Possibly the children will find new friends and interests at Schatzheim, and their relationship with their mother will dwindle out. Or perhaps the grandmother will become so attached to the children that she will assume a larger role and join them. And it is even possible, though not likely, that AR will mature, rebuild her life, and rejoin her children.

The four cases above offer a bird's eye view of Schatzheim, but to really know the place a reader needs to vicariously join a family like the Oelkers, to live there with them and experience the place first hand on many levels. No former Schatzheim resident has become president yet, it is true. But one of them may, they may.

Future Farmers

In December, 1999, Minnesota public television presented "Death of the Dream," a disturbing but popular program that chronicled the demise of the family farm. This feature, based in part on William Gabler's book, traced a mournful trail through photos and footage of abandoned Minnesota farmsteads—remnants of the culture and economic system that dominated America when we were young.

Dreams end, but life does not. Despite the greatest catastrophe, it continues to build palaces and hovels on the ashes of the past. What economic system, and what culture, will produce food in the future? Will our "Cheap Food Policy" die with the rest of the dream? Perhaps it isn't even a policy, but merely an artifact. And perhaps food isn't actually cheap anyway. The farmer's share of the food dollar has shrunk to insignificance, but the costs of advertising, packaging, and processing have burgeoned.

Perhaps, perhaps, perhaps. Perhaps, against all expectations, a new and better culture will replace the vaunted human values of rural America. Perhaps common sense will combine with economics, technology, public awareness, and government regulation to produce a new agriculture that is friendly to the environment, the consumer, and the farmer. Again, perhaps not.
What follows is speculation about a form that the world of agriculture might take in the future. No one can know what will actually happen, of course, but here is a possibility based on the agricultural history of the past century, much of which

I have experienced directly or through my parents and grandparents.

Anything we say about the future is, in a sense, fictional, so I have cast this speculation in the form of a story. It seemed to be the best way to discuss the human, as well as the technological, aspects of the revolution in farming. The story is set a few decades out into the future at some indeterminate location in the farm country of southern Minnesota and northern Iowa, and follows ordinary people as they live and work in a new world of agriculture. *************

One Town, One Church, One School

Two girls bound for St. Louis attended to their nails and listened to music as their small plane, guided by satellite, droned its way across southern Minnesota and Iowa. Below them, unattended machines crawled across vast fields of corn and soybeans. There were no houses or signs of habitation except for an occasional cluster of industrial buildings. Small cities were spaced perhaps twenty-five miles apart. A few cars and trucks moved along a sparse road net that separated the huge fields from each other, and there was traffic on the highways that connected the cities.

"What are they actually doing down there, hon?"

"I dunno. Growing corn and stuff, I guess. I've heard my grandpa talking about it, and I remember we had to read about it in school."

"But what makes those machines go along those rows, and keeps the rows so straight clear across those big fields? That machine over there is even going right across a little pond of water. And how big are those fields anyway?"

"Well, duh. I don't remember all that. Punch up the aircraft channel button on the internet there. They'll have some smart ass ready to tell you more about it than you really want to know. But it's interactive, so you can butt in and ask questions. He'll know where we are and be able to see pretty much what we're looking at."

"The fields are a thousand acres or larger," said an unctuous voice. "Generally they are a mile or two across. The machines are pulled by steel cables and guided by radio. Observe the large round objects at each end of the row the machine is traversing. Those are reels of steel cable. The cable winds and unwinds from the reels to pull the machine back and forth across the field, and a radio signal guides it along a straight line between them. When ---"

The girl's manicured finger hit the "talk" button impatiently. "But the pond of water?"

The voice continued with scarcely a pause, as if the question had kicked it into an instantaneous fast forward to a new part of a prepared spiel. "Since the machines have no need for heavy motors or transmissions, they can be made to be very light in weight. They also have very large balloon tires, so they can float across mud and water. It allows them to work night and day, and in all kinds of weather. The cables carry electricity too, so the machines have electric motors, hydraulic pistons, TV cameras and other accessories."

The girls switched off, and sat back to study the scene below.

"Hmm. It's kinda pretty, you know. Huge open fields of nothing but corn—not a tree, not a building, not a road. But then each field is surrounded by wide, irregular borders of trees, streams, roads, and hills. It's like art on a really big scale."

"Yeah, but it sure looks lonesome. The monitor says that little town there is called Ansbach. What would it be like to live in Ansbach?"

A lonesome-ass ten hours on the farm coming up, thought Steve Zinnel as he wheeled his pickup out of Ansbach at 3:30 on a hot July afternoon. I'll be glad to get back on days next week; it seems as if I never get any sleep when I'm pullin' this damn four to two.

He had said the exact same thing that morning when Beth's alarm clock jangled them awake at 6:30. She was snuggled against him, and he was dreaming about a swimming date they had back in high school.

"Tell me I don't have to get up for a while yet," she murmured.

"Well, O.K., but you'll have to tell the kids to get their own breakfast and then call the school so they can line up a substitute teacher for you."

"Spoilsport," she answered, sliding away from him and swinging her legs out from beneath the covers. Her toes searched for slippers beside the bed.

"Well, how about me?" Steve complained. "I was dreaming about that time down at the Mermaid Plunge. Besides, I feel as if I just got to bed. I'll be glad to get back on days next week; it seems as if I never get any sleep when I'm pullin' this damn four to two."

Beth had a different take. "You'd get enough sleep if you'd come home when you get off, instead of slopping up beer at that damned bar."

"Geez. Big deal. I had two beers and a sandwich."

She grinned and came around to kiss him on the forehead. "Go back to sleep," she said.

She had a point about the bar, he supposed, but he didn't drink much or stay long. You couldn't—not with this job. Farming a two-thousand acre field by remote control was tense, demanding work. Thousands of dollars often hung on his every move, and the corporation demanded ten-hour shifts, and six shifts a week, during the growing season. So most operators had the habit of stopping at Maggie's at 2:30 a.m. to unwind, tell war stories, and compare notes.

"Seminars," he told Beth.

"Seminoles, you mean," she shot back, referring to an exotic dancer who had gained notoriety in a neighboring town a few years earlier. But Beth was interested in hearing about the tips and stories he gleaned from other operators. Her own relationship with them was somewhat aloof. They were smart and skillful, but she saw them as a strange bunch—alien to the regular world.

It was lonely, edgy work. The closest parallel, it was said, was terraforming. But that was science fiction, and these were real machines—and real dollars too. Steve had to push hard every minute to meet production goals, but they were all over him if he screwed up the crop, or broke anything, or did something to pollute the environment.

"Those science fiction jokers seem to have carte blanche compared to me," Steve mused. "They've always got control of an army of robotic machines down on some uninhabitable planet somewhere, trying to build an earth-like island, and they lay into it slam bang, but if they screw it up too bad they just scrap the whole project and move on. I wouldn't last a week if I took the risks they do."

Part of Beth's reservations about Steve's associates stemmed from a feeling that they shared, in all too great a measure, the cavalier attitude of their science fiction counterparts. "That woman operator he's working with now, that Barbara Martin, always acts as though she'd be happy to gamble the whole state of Iowa on a roll of the dice," Beth often thought. She was impatient with provincial Ansbach, and wanted to be out in the world. She taught in Ansbach's only school—kindergarten through twelfth grade under one roof. Ansbach was the county seat too, although there wasn't much need for county government. The countryside was corporate turf, everyone lived in town, and Ansbach County, like many counties, only had one town. One town, one city hall/courthouse, one library, one school. One church, too, although it was used by several church groups. One of everything, it seemed, except for grain elevators and crop storage silos—oodles of those and a good railroad track to serve them. The corporations didn't sell until they got their price.

Beth wanted Steve to leave the corporation—to stop being a farm operator and find a city job. In St. Cloud, maybe, where she could advance her own career. She had an advanced degree and innovation was sweeping the field of public education, but it would never happen in this one-horse town with its one-room-per-grade setup. And what was this antiquated, primitive system doing to their kids?

But Steve snorted when she mentioned St. Cloud. "Ha!" he said. "I was through there a few weeks ago and stopped at a fast food place for a burger and a coke. Fifteen dollars and something."

"Well, it's not much different here, or anyplace else; your Ag corporations have seen to that. Six-fifty for a half gallon of milk now, and almost thirteen dollars for a box of cereal."

"Yeah. Well, food is still pretty damn reasonable, compared to everything else. Anyway, I didn't make the system; I just work here."

"Well, you could work someplace else, you know. Someplace where everybody in town doesn't have to know every time you take a shit. One of the other teachers stopped me in the hall yesterday to ask if everything was all right. She thought she had seen your mother's car in town."

Steve smiled. "So what did you tell her?"

Steve's mother did drive out from Chicago for a couple of days from time to time. She brought books, which she read while the family went about its business. One night, near bedtime, she looked up from her book. "It says here that small towns are being reborn," she said. "Is Ansbach reborn?"

Steve laughed. "Reborn is a funny word for it. They usually compare us to the small towns of a hundred years ago."

Beth jumped instantly into the conversation. "When it comes to being nosy, we've got everything those towns had except the party line, and we might as well have that too."

"Well, yeah," Steve nodded. "I guess they were provincial, and we are too. But those towns were spaced about five miles apart and provided services for the farm families who lived between them. These towns now are more like twenty-five miles apart, and nobody lives between them. The town people are the farmers. Except for a few people like you—schoolteachers, storekeepers, and whatnot—practically every working person in Ansbach works for one or another of the Ag corporations."

"I wish you'd stop talking like you were reading from some damn textbook," answered Beth. "You do that all the time. You sound like a robot."

Steve grimaced. "Maybe it's an occupational hazard. A lot of our machines are voice-activated. It's nice, but you have to be really careful about what you say. Machines don't care how you feel or what you really mean, one way or the other. The only thing that's counts is what you say or do."

"I saw a movie in Chicago a while ago about how there used to be company towns around the coal mines," said Steve's mother, trying to get the conversation back on subject. "Ansbach doesn't seem to be much like them though."

"No, it's not. The corporations don't own Ansbach."

Beth spoke again. "From what I've read, those old small towns had it all over us in one way. They were permanent. People were born there, lived there, and died there. Ansbach is so transient. Five years from now, most of these people will have been transferred out, and a different bunch will be here."

"Yeah. Beth's right there, Mom. A U.S. military dependent housing complex in a foreign country would be about the most similar kind of a community."

Beth had the last word. "So why in the hay are we here then?"

It was a good question. Although they had been in Ansbach less than ten years, the Zinnels were seen as old settlers. The corporations tried to cooperate with the towns to keep teachers and other community leaders in place. Steve's job specialty had a role too—he was a farm operator. A mechanic can work anywhere, but the corporation didn't need farm operators at their Chicken and Egg Division down in West Virginia.

School was in session, so Beth was still at work when Steve left the house. He had spent some time in the garden and sprayed the apple tree after he got up at 10:30. He also went down to Menard's, the only building supply store in town, to look at paint. He and Beth had agreed on a color, a matte finish ivory, and his intention was to get the house painted this summer. It was a two-story colonial, and wasn't bad yet, but he didn't want to let it go too far.

The better quality latex was on sale at fifty dollars a gallon, so he loaded eight one-gallon cans into the pickup, and bought a new trim brush. Shift work was good in one respect, it put him home at different times of the day, so he could arrange to always paint in the shade—you got a better job that way.

Leaving before Beth got home seemed like a lonesome thing to do, especially today when the kids had baseball scheduled after school. He barely got to see them, and they were busy getting ready for the game anyway.

School in July seemed odd to city dwellers, but it was a good idea. The corporations were liberal with vacation, but you had to take it in the winter. As a result, in places like Ansbach, the traditional three-month school vacation came in January, February, and March.

There was little traffic as Steve tooled along the hot paved highway on his way to work, and his mind returned to those conversations with Beth. Why was he working for the corporation, and why were they living in Ansbach?

One answer was obvious. You didn't give up a good job lightly, not if you were a family man. Beth's salary was important to the family finances, but he was the major breadwinner. She assumed he could get a good job in the city, but he was not so sure. Living expenses were high as it was, and college for the kids was looming ahead.

A cock pheasant, resplendent in iridescent colors, burst from a patch of sunflowers beside the road as the pickup approached, and stormed off to the northeast, away from the sun. The fields were sterile, but wildlife flourished in the border areas. Steve's eye followed the pheasant as his mind raced ahead of it to the city, where Beth thought a better job awaited her. Maybe so, but maybe not, too. The explosive growth of St. Cloud had brought new immigrants and rafts of social problems, in and out of the schools.

These were reasons for caution, but there were larger questions too. Where was the good life in America now?

Talk about the "good old days" of farming still lingered, and it was easy to get lost in that argument. Was corporate farming, and the stability it provided, a good or a bad thing? What about the loss of access to the countryside for city people? And how about the loss of the old way of life, and all of that? Steve didn't know, and couldn't really know. It was a life he had never experienced, and it was gone anyway.

But he knew Ansbach. Beth says our schools are antiquated, he mused, and that our kids, coming from here, are going to feel like freaks when they get out into the world, but I think she exaggerates. It seems to me that the kids are doing very well.

Ansbach residents and their kind were rare birds, though. Not one person in a thousand was a farmer, and the very existence of farming was almost unknown to most people. After the general public had been shut off from the countryside they had nearly forgotten there was such a place. If they wanted to experience the outdoors, they had parks and public land. And, as Steve was fond of saying, they always had their golf courses.

Ansbach had a golf course too. Like everything else there, it was simple and bare bones. But what the hell. A lot of the people lived in simple apartments, rather than in a house like Steve and Beth did, but the apartments were well kept. Almost everything in town, actually, was pretty well taken care of—there were no slums in Ansbach. The "Lifers"—school teachers, merchants, and a few retired people—dominated city government, and they ran a tight ship. Others just came and went, and followed the rules.

His beeper squawked and brought him out of his reverie when he swung off the highway onto the corporate road net. It showed that the computer had picked him up. He still had eight miles to go to reach the field they were working, but the computer would notify Matt that he was on the way in.

Matt's Audi was in the tractor shed; he often pulled it in there to keep it out of the sun, although there was supposed to be some kind of a rule against doing so. Steve and Matt and Barbara Martin were the three operators working this field right now. The ten hour shifts gave them a two hour overlap. Matt would leave at six, and then Steve would be alone until Barbara came in at midnight. Truckers and mechanics came and went, along with supervisors and engineers, but there were many days when Steve spent six hours alone with two thousand acres of ground—and a hell of a lot of machinery.

The work was intense, and he felt wrung out at the end of a shift, but the time passed quickly. Steve had developed a habit of listening to Handel or Vivaldi as he worked, and had become adept at patching in appropriate passages so the music orchestrated the plunging, clicking, crawling, and turning of his machines. In the wee, still hours before midnight he had been known to turn from his console to bow to an imaginary audience in the darkened, cobwebby recesses of a cavernous barn while a crescendo from the Hallelujah Chorus died to a whisper, and the corn planter turned ponderously at the end of a row to head off across the field toward a full moon, low in the western sky.

The midnight shift was especially lonely; you seldom saw anybody through those six hours of sitting there guiding machines up and down invisible rows in the dark. People marveled that they could follow the rows so well in the dark, but actually the dark had nothing to do with it. Neither the machine nor the operator even looked at the row on the ground for guidance. The machine precisely followed a line established by radio signals from the cable spools at each end of the row, and didn't vary from it by more than an inch in the entire two mile trip across the field.

When the fields had been set up, bulldozers had removed all trees, ditches, buildings, and other obstacles. They also reduced any steep slopes to the point that the farming machines could accurately control and position themselves. The ruthless preparation of these huge, factory-like, fields created enormous resentment at the time, Steve had read. Roads, stately groves of trees, centennial family farmsteads, and even towns, were swept away without a trace. But that was history. Now, Steve's computer regularly updated a soil map that carried the chemical composition and fertilizer requirements of every square yard of this gigantic field, and his machines chose the plant food for every spot as carefully as William Butler Yeats chose the words for his immortal verses.

The advent of all-weather machinery had spurred the geneticists to develop frost-resistant varieties that matured rapidly, so two crops in a year from a field had become normal. Steve and his crew had just taken the beans off of this field, and they were putting it back into a new forage crop. The job would be done by the end of the next week, and the operators would move on to a new field somewhere. Steve hoped he wouldn't get stuck with a long drive or an out-of-town assignment. The corporation was opening up a bunch of new fields in Kansas, and he had been sent down there for three weeks one time last year. The union forced the corporation to pay a bonus for that kind of work, but most operators hated it anyway.

Otherwise, Steve didn't much care where he was assigned. One field was a lot like another. Different sizes and shapes, of course, and hills were still a problem in a few places, but mostly, seated at the console, he could almost forget which field he was working.

It was different when he had a chance to actually get out on the ground. Out there, every field, every spot on the ground, every plant, every odor, was unique. You could look at the soil, sift it through your fingers, taste it, and smell it. You could watch and smell the miracle of the development of each ear of corn, each kernel. Out there, he felt, you knew something of farming as it once was.

But such experiences were rare. These fields seldom saw the imprint of a human foot. Steve's corporation did still use free moving tractors with drivers to tow the wagons in during harvest, but an extra crew came for that, and Steve was usually busy at his console anyway, controlling the harvesting machine and the unloading operation.

The corporation had been trying to develop equipment that would eliminate the need for the tractor crew at harvest, and Steve had worked with the new system during the three weeks he had spent in Kansas. It involved a double cable setup that towed a train of small wagons. It worked in dry weather if there were no ponds, but it was hard to get enough floatation for that much weight if you had to cross wet ground. Free moving tractors didn't have to go in straight lines, so they could avoid the wet areas.

Another corporation was experimenting with a different idea—free moving, but unmanned, tractors operated by remote control. An interesting idea, he thought, but they had better have something out-of-the-ordinary in the way of a control system for those puppies. He could envision tractors with loaded wagons crashing into each other or into the harvesting machine or getting lost and heading resolutely off across country in all directions—through fences and lakes, over roads and whatnot. Ugh. Pity the poor operator who was trying to handle all of that, plus what he had already.

In due time, as snow began to dust the ground, the final crops were harvested and the fields were tilled and laid by for winter. Training and equipment maintenance became big items, and Steve spent two weeks in Argentina in December to help the corporation train some new operators there. He got home three days before Christmas, just as school closed for the year. Beth and the kids were off for three months, and the corporation always had a ten-day Christmas holiday, so it was family time. Not only that—Steve had scheduled his four-week vacation to start in mid-January, and they were going to Fiji. The Zinnels were on a roll.

They drove to Chicago for a big family gathering at Christmas, and Beth's California sister and her family came to Ansbach for a few days after that. Beth and Steve declared a Christmas season moratorium on the argument about their future, with the understanding that they would thresh it out while they were in Fiji.

"Sounds like a hell of a way to spend a vacation," said Beth's sister when Beth confided in her about the plan.

"I suppose it does, in a way," she answered. "But we have to work this out, and I think we need a place where we have time together and aren't being pressed. The kids have a million plans for snorkeling, fishing, jungle rides, dances, and I don't know what all, so Steve and I are thinking there'll be a lot of time when we can sit on the beach, sip Margaritas, and talk. He says that if we can find a spot to set up our chairs and umbrella a little ways back from the water where the native girls take the sun, he doesn't see why we'd have to move around much."

"The dog. You may have trouble keeping his mind on the conversation. I understand that practically all of them go topless down there."

Fiji was a far cry from the frozen cornfields of northern Iowa. "I think you're trying to soften me up with this," Beth said as they sat over a late breakfast on the hotel veranda. "All of that tenseness, worry, and irritation seems as if it's a million miles away."

"I know it. I've almost forgotten what soybeans even are. "

"The funny thing is, we've sort of become celebrities here," mused Beth.

"Ain't that the truth. Most of these tourists have never talked with a farmer before, so they are a little bit fascinated by us. The old ideals of farming and farm life still have a kind of a romantic appeal. Embedded in the American culture, I guess."

"Easy enough for them," said Beth. "They aren't embedded in Ansbach."

"Ansbach's not so bad. A lot of places are worse."

The argument wore on, neither of them willing to capitulate. Beth had been offered a job in the St. Paul school system. The thought of a job and a life away from the tedium and provincialism of Ansbach thrilled her, and the kids were dying for the new adventure.

Beth had never told Steve about it, but she was also still uncomfortable about Steve's work and his co-workers. They were so engrossed in their work that they seemed to constitute a cult— an impenetrable cult. She was on the outside, looking in. Not even able to look in, really. She liked to have control, but there was something here she could not control, and she felt threatened by it. "Why can't he go and get a civilized, regular job like everybody else?" she blustered to herself.

"A move would screw up the school year for the kids," Steve pointed out. "They'd be switching into a system that has summer vacation. Who even knows what grade they'd be put in?" But Beth had done her homework, and had good answers for all questions like that.

Most of all, Steve thought it would be hard to find another job that would pay as well as the one he had, or be as interesting. Truth to tell, Steve liked Ansbach, he liked his job, and he didn't like the city.

Finally, in desperation and with great foreboding, Beth suggested a compromise. Hugging her knees, staring at her toes, feeling as if she was stepping off into a perilous unknown, and speaking in a low and careful voice, she said: "Actually, St. Paul isn't all that far. Maybe the kids and I should move there and you should stay in Ansbach. We could still be together on weekends, holidays, and vacations, and that's about the only time we ever see you during season anyway."

Steve stirred on his chair as a deep twinge passed through his abdomen. Life without Beth and the kids was not something he wanted to contemplate, and this seemed like an ominous step in that direction. "You're exaggerating," he said. "I'm gone a lot, but it's not that bad. I do a lot of things with the kids, and I help them with their homework. I think they would miss that. I know I would."

"Yes, they would miss you a lot, and so would I. That's very hard for me. But we would still have a lot of time together. I don't know if you understand, Steve. I feel as if I'm fighting for my life, and for the kids, and for our marriage. I feel as if I can't control it anymore. If I don't get a chance to try this I'll just continue to get more witchy than I already am. We've got to do something."

"What about the house? I don't know if we can afford two houses. Besides that, I wouldn't have time to take care of it alone. We'd have to sell it. Think of all of the work and money we've put into the house and yard, and of how much we all like the place— It's home."

"I know, and I almost cry about it. But we've got to do something."

"Worst of all, what if you get up there and you or the kids don't like it? What then? Where would you go next? What would we do?"

Silence over knitted brows and tearful eyes. Finally: "Maybe we could do it as an experiment for a year. I'm sure we could rent the house; there's a good market. Could you stand to stay in a rented room or a studio apartment for that time? You wouldn't be there much anyway." She looked beseechingly at the side of his stony face while he studied a crack in the sidewalk. A full minute passed.

"Okay then," he said, as he put his arms around her shaking shoulders and hugged her to him.

A few months later, on a July morning, another small plane droned its way over Ansbach. Surprised to see a busy school and a quiet town in July, its occupants circled for a closer look.

Only one house, a matte finish, ivory-colored, two-story colonial, was an exception to the general torpor. Moving vans, cars and pickups were clustered around it and a dozen or more people were rushing about. Some were carrying stuff out of the house and loading it onto a van or parking it on the lawn. Others were unloading another van and taking stuff into the house.

"Looks like moving day, and a tight schedule," said the pilot with a laugh.

"Yeah, hit the internet there. The information it has is unreal. I'll bet they could even tell us who's moving out and who's moving in."

"The information you request is private," answered a tinny voice. "Please enter your official NTK (Need to know) code."

On the ground, the mood was more tense. Steve stood beside his pickup, staring glumly at its meager load of his clothes and a few household items and tools that he was taking to his little studio apartment on the east edge of town. Most of his stuff, and indeed much of the household, had been sold at a garage sale the previous week. The condo where Beth and the kids would live in St. Paul was, while much larger than his studio, still too small to hold the accumulation of years that had been in the house.

Beth was making an unconvincing show of brisk efficiency as she supervised the loading of the moving van, but she was biting her tongue and fighting back tears most of the time. On one final trip through the house, as her footsteps echoed through their empty bedroom, she broke down completely, hid her face against the wall, and wailed in misery.

The kids were quiet and ill at ease. They sensed a great problem, a breakdown in communication between their parents, and it was an overwhelming experience for them.

Finally the van door was closed and the driver was in his seat ready to follow Beth's car to St. Paul. As new beds and sofas began to move into the empty house, the Zinnels stood together in their driveway beside the car and the pickup for the last time. It seemed like a parting, but they made a point of not saying goodbye.

"Well, I suppose we'd better get started," said Beth. "The van driver is waiting, and I'd like to get there and get this stuff into the condo and located before tonight."

"Yeah, I suppose so," answered Steve.

"We'll see you on Sunday, then?"

"Yeah, unless something comes up. I'll be working until two a.m.,so I may just drive on up there after I get off work. It'd put me in there about four or five on Sunday morning.

"Okay, good. You've got a key, so we won't wait up."

"Now you kids remember, you've got work to do when you get there," added Steve, hugging one of them around the neck with each arm in a gesture of mock severity. "Don't go running off somewhere. Stay in the house and help your mother with this stuff. You can look around later."

"Okay, Dad," they said. It seemed to help.

As Ben Franklin Once Said

Benjamin Franklin attributed much of the joy, and the success, of his life to The Junto, a reading, writing, and talking club that met every Friday evening, starting in 1727 when he was 21, and continuing for nearly forty years. The club was, he said:

> The best School of Philosophy, and Politics that then existed in the Province; for our Queries which were read the Week preceding their Discussion, put us on reading with Attention upon the several Subjects, that we might speak more to the purpose; and here too we acquired better Habits of Conversation, everything being studied in our Rules which might prevent our disgusting each other.

Like Franklin, I get great satisfaction from an opportunity to participate in a learned discussion—a discussion where the participants are able and ready to bring something worthwhile to the argument—as most people can, given a suitable forum. The Junto had rules to ensure that the discussion was carried out in the "sincere Spirit of Enquiry after Truth, without Fondness for Dispute, or Desire of Victory." With an attitude like that, and with some prior preparation or thought, almost anyone can contribute something worthwhile to most topics, because everyone has ideas.

Sex, liquor, food, and other physical things are of great consequence for us, but ideas, more than anything else, make us what we are. We have ideas about kindness, ideas about compassion, ideas about courage, and ideas about revenge. We have ideas about education, ideas about government, ideas about astronomy, and ideas about football. The list is endless.

These ideas are crammed into books, newspapers, and magazines; we see them presented on television or at the movies in various ways, and hear them talked about from the pulpit or on the radio. The modern world is suffused with talking heads and printing presses. The ideas may be as complex as quantum mechanics or as simple as a bodily function,; the message may be direct, inferred, or hidden, the presentation may be via the simple spoken word or via fantastic, elaborate special effects, but always, the presenter is attempting to convey some idea to his listener or viewer. In advertising, the idea being conveyed is simply that the listener or viewer will be happier if she or he buysthe presenter's product or service. But other ideas, important ideas, complex ideas, are presented elsewhere—perhaps in a book, perhaps in a lecture, perhaps in some other way.

For the readers, listeners, or viewers, these are passive activities. They sit and absorb the ideas while someone else talks—an efficient and indispensable mode of communicating ideas.

Lecturers, however, often have an agenda—some unspoken bias, some tendancy to stress a particular point of view while ignoring or minimizing others, some interest that lends a bias to his presentation. When I listen to a lecture, often after years of hearing other "takes" on the same subject, I often yearn to see or hear someone interrupt the lecturer with a good "Yeah, but . . . .." Lecture, despite its many merits, is no substitute for debate and discussion. We need both.

Fortunately for me, I have three places where I regularly sit in on good discussions. So I say that I have three suns—that I am thrice blessed.

One group meets at a local library at 10:00 am each Friday, and operates in much the same way as Franklin's Junto did. The library is good enough to furnish us with a conference room and an urn of coffee, so we go from there. Officially, for reasons I won't attempt to explain, we are called Café Philo, but my son, with tongue in cheek and a sly look in his eye, refers to us as "your wise man's group." Strictly speaking, he is wrong because women are welcome and sometimes do come, as do a few younger men, but the core group does consist of about ten retired men. Topics are set a week in advance so we can, and do, prepare to some extent, but the main thrust is to try to apply any collective experience and learning we have to the topic at hand.

Our club is fortunate in its membership in that, when a factual question arises, there is usually someone at the table who can give a reasonably good account of how many stars there are in the Milky Way, or of the viral nature of certain ulcers, or of what Kepler said to Galileo, or Diogenes to Alexander. Someone else can explain how the second law of thermodynamics applies to the construction of the building across the street, or knows a Somali family and their wedding customs. Likewise, if our discussion of the value of athletics turns to a comparison of the place of athletics in our culture vs. that of ancient Rome, and someone asks to have this comparison extended to some Eastern culture, there will probably be someone who has some knowledge of the Han Dynasty of China, which was concurrent with, and somewhat similar to, the Roman Empire. Such questions are never the central topic, but they do arise in the discussion. Some recent topics the group has considered follow:

The Value of Athletics

Victims

Charity vs. Government programs

Was Lincoln Right?

Why has "liberal" become a dirty word?

Responsibility for children (State vs. Parent)

How safe are we?

Southeast Asia

What is a fair tax?

Leadership

The Space Program

The European Union

We have been meeting for several years, so a complete list would be long.

142 – At the Oasis

Occasionally, someone at Philo will suggest that we ought to have so-and-so come in and talk to us about a topic we are scheduled to discuss, because she or he is a real expert in it. We have tried this idea (listening to a lecture by an expert), but it doesn't work out well. If George Bush offered to come and speak to us, we would probably accept out of courtesy to his position, or out of ego at the honor, but we have all heard Mr. Bush before, many times; and sitting and listening is not what we normally do. We would be impatient with sound bites, and would want to urge him on to some statement of substance, and then interrupt him and relegate him to the sidelines while we went around the table and commented in turn about the shortcomings, strengths, and implications of his idea.

In a similar way, we would be uncomfortable and impatient if the president turned to berating his political enemies or questioning their motives. We like to see ideas attacked or supported on their merits, not on the basis of who holds them, or claims to hold them. Hitler's ideas on fair taxation would be of as much interest to us as those of the pope. George Bush would probably feel compelled to react with horror and scorn to any suggestion that Hitler had any good ideas about anything, but we do not, and we do not accuse one another of a lack of appreciation of the horror and evil of the Holocaust as a result of some suggestion that there was merit in Germany's method of sponsoring research in her universities.

Discussions like ours are only possible if intemperance is held in check. Philo is not a place to rage at the Devil or resort to tears. Controversial or unpopular ideas are welcome at the table, although they may emerge in tatters. What we favor is reasoned, comfortable controversy. In general, we prefer the abstract to the personal, and our discussions usually succeed the best when several points of view emerge.

A pair of new words has come into use recently; or at least this use is new to me. I have been hearing about horizontal conversations and about their comparison to vertical conversations. The problem in Iraq in recent years has been that all of the conversation has been vertical, it is said. Top down, in that case of course, although a vertical conversation could also be bottom up. The Iraqi people, perhaps from fear, had formed the habit of merely listening to their officials and doing as they were told, according to this view. Reporters on the scene claim that a problem facing the institution of democracy in Iraq is that the people there have not had significant conversations with each other for years, and consequently, no longer know how to do so.

I don't know if this is so or not, but the "vertical vs. horizontal" dichotomy does seem to come close to expressing the same thing I have been saying about the merits of discussion and debate as compared to lecture. Vertical vs. horizontal, however, implies a structure. For the idea to be meaningful there has to be a top and a bottom and communication between them that is different from communication between those on the same level. But such "top down" communication is just a special case of a scenario where the reader or listener assumes a passive role and just sits and listens. He could equally well do that from a speaker or writer at his own level, so horizontal conversation would not necessarily be participatory, which is probably what those reporters in Iraq really find lacking. Iraq needs, as do we, a combination of passive and active modes, of lecture and discussion, as well as horizontal and vertical discourse.

In its own small way, Philo serves the same purpose for us as the Junto served for Franklin and his associates, and an extension of it to Baghdad might serve that country well.

"Old age is a privilege accorded to only a select few."

Cutter told me that. He spoke one morning while we were polishing off our eggs and toast at the Oasis. It happened to be LaVerne's 79th birthday, so that's how the subject came up. I was surprised to hear such an astute remark from a man so young. Cutter is about the age of my kids—not yet fifty, I would guess. He also gives me advice about the operation and maintenance of my skid steer Caterpillar tractor, a topic where his expertise far exceeds mine.

This is my second sun—another discussion group, similar in nature to Philo, if different in outward appearance. Membership is an even less formal concept here—just whoever happens to be having breakfast at the counter in the Oasis Café. The conversation often drifts to hunting, football, and the weather, but weightier topics are considered as well. Club Philo abounds with doctors, scientists, teachers, judges, ministers, and engineers, while the group at the Oasis runs more to farmers, truck drivers, factory workers, mechanics, carpenters, and construction people, but the essence of the dialog is often amazingly similar. Both groups seem to delight in a sort of intellectual curiosity that I find to be irresistible. They want to get to the bottom of things, and they delve into the news, their own experiences, and what learning they have for parallels. Relatively speaking, of course, "book learning" plays a larger role at Philo, but actually the speaker's personal experiences, and his reaction to them, play the dominant role in both groups. These guys have a lively interest in everything from foreign policy to discipline in the schools. They read and listen, they've been there and done that, and they have ideas about it.

But I said three suns. The third one is a bit unusual. Despite the fact that I am over eighty, I take classes at the university in Mankato, Minnesota. I am, in a sense, Young Man Axelbrod, the sixty-five year old backwoods Scandinavian farmer created—and sent to Yale—by Sinclair Lewis in 1917. Like him, I sometimes view my college experiences with a puzzled eye, but each of us also found much that was new and fascinating there. In my case, I take graduate level courses in English, sometimes in English Literature, but mostly in Creative Writing. To get in, I had to take some remedial courses to compensate for my very non-English major background (physics, law, and military). Axelbrod got in (barely) by passing entrance exams. I don't know that Yale would let him do that today, but I assume it was possible then—Lewis would know; he went there and had the same complaints about the place that he put into the mouth of Axelbrod.

Most graduate-level writing classes are not classes in the conventional sense—they are called workshops, and meet once a week for about three hours. My main activities there are reading and critiquing the writing of the other students in the class and having my own writing, in turn, read and critiqued by my fellow students and by the professor. So there is lots of discussion. The class will typically spend an hour or so on a particular story or essay and somewhat less on a poem.

Lots of discussion, but the discussions are very different from those at Philo or at the Oasis. Writing classes stress the process of writing—writing as a craft. A writer worthy of the name ought to be able to write about whatever needs to be written about—that's the idea. The topic is, in a sense, secondary. Certainly, for some writers—newspaper reporters for example—this is indubitably true. For others it may be less true, but all good writers have to master the craft, so this is what writing classes concentrate on, and what we, as students, discuss when we critique each other's work.

If an author presents an essay in which she or he champions some particular position about the value of athletics, we do not debate the substance of this argument as we would at Philo or at the Oasis. Instead, we ask if she communicates clearly, if his grammar is error free, if she makes the subject interesting—draws her reader in. We ask if he has immersed himself in the world of athletics sufficiently to know what he is talking about, and, if so, does his voice have enough authority so that his reader will trust what he says? We look at the way she has structured her essay, we speculate whether or not some other structure might work better, and we mercilessly probe any facts he may offer to make sure they are really factual. So we have a lively time.

At Philo, or at the Oasis, the same essay would draw an equally lively response, but in entirely different terms. Defenders would note that athletics develops the essential skill of teamwork, and teaches the importance of rules to participants and to spectators alike. Each of us might offer specific instances from his life, or from history, or perhaps from literature, that seem to demonstrate this idea in action, or perhaps reveal it to have been counter productive in some instance. Detractors of the jock culture would decry the over-emphasis on school sports at the expense of academic achievement or other extra curricular activities, and offer specific examples from their experience or from their reading. College football and basketball teams are simply professional athletes in disguise, few athletes actually go on to get a degree, someone would say. Maybe so, but they draw in crowds and make the money that supports a host of other sports, someone else would reply, and would cite statistics from the Big Ten to support his view.

And so it would go, from player salaries to stadiums, from jock culture to Title IX. Title IX, though well-intentioned, has created some strange situations such as a women's rowing team at the arid University of Arizona. Voices would rise and hours would pass until the clock put an end to the fight, at least for that day.

So, for good reason, at Mankato we argue the process of writing, while at the Oasis and at Philo we pass directly to the substance of the topic. Actually though, at all three places, there is another important element of process at work during the argument. Discussion would be impossible without a certain amount of self-discipline. One cannot simply blather on; others are waiting to speak. Short, pithy, statements find favor, especially at the Oasis. Long, passionate outbursts are anathema. Think it through, have something to say, say it, and get out—this is the structure that finds favor during discussion, whether at Philo, or at Mankato, or at the Oasis. As Franklin put it so bluntly, we don't want to disgust each other.

Being part of a writer's group can be a devastating experience, but it is also a fascinating one. It always seems to me to have something in common with what I understand to be the methods of group therapy, such as at Alcoholics Anonymous. There are few other places where a person's inner mind is the center of attention of a group to the degree that it is while that person's writing is being worked over at a writer's workshop.

But the experience of writing is not, of course, confined to those who participate in workshops. Writing has a peculiar fascination of its own, partly because it is such a solitary activity. My experience, and that of many, is that we never really understand a topic until we try to write about it. Franklin's Junto was different from our Café Philo in this respect—Junto members were expected to produce and share essays on the topic of the day. To write about a topic well, the writer has to try to carry on the whole Café Philo discussion within her or his own head, and more. She also has to organize the material in a coherent manner and research the topic adequately to be sure that no major facets of it are ignored.

A writer expects his essay or other piece of writing to be examined critically, in detail, and over time, by many readers who expect it to give a reasonably complete and comprehensive account of whatever subject it treats. So Philo probably does not cover its topics as well or as completely as Junto did. A really thorough treatment of a topic needs both the freedom of discussion and the discipline of writing.

At Mankato we write, but then I often find that I wish we had time to also discuss the substance of the essays—to consider the merits of the ideas presented, as well as the merit of the presentation. I long there for the type of discussion we have at Philo and at the Oasis. It seems to me that, ultimately, any writing will be judged partly on the strength of the ideas it presents. But of course, to discuss our work in that manner would require far more time than we have available. Learning about ideas, discussing them, exploring them, is in a sense what a student's whole college experience is, or at least should be, about.

The complaint of Axelbrod and Sinclair Lewis about Yale was a contention that the college experience there was not about ideas—that the trend there, and by implication, in universities generally, was to steer clear of discussions of ideas—that a sort of anti-intellectualism had taken root in our academic institutions, and that many people there pursue, at best, their own narrow specialties.

My own college experience is too limited to allow me to join in such a sweeping indictment, and most of a century has passed since Axelbrod attended Yale, but I must say that I still see traces of the problems that Lewis describes. My poems are too "thinky," I was told by my professor in a course on the prose poem. A student in another course roundly denounced one of my poems for a reference it made to The Angkor Wat. "Write about things we know something about," he snorted. His own poems (which were admittedly superior to mine) concentrated on fruit in the refrigerator—pears, cold plums, peaches. I liked his poems, but I often wondered where he would go after he hit zucchini.

It is in poetry, surprisingly, that we may be seeing a new trend—a moderation of what some see as a fixation on self and feeling in favor of a trend toward more argument and idea. Modern poets have long been accused of having abandoned their natural audience in favor of writing for each other, but today's anti-war movement may be transforming them. Poets Against the War readings have spread across the country—politics has come back into poetry. Perhaps "thinky" poems and prose will yet find favor. Ben Franklin and Sinclair Lewis will both be proud of us.

A Dangerous Idea

Originally published:
Minnesota Literature
Volume 28, No. 4, December 2002
1st Place, MN Lit. Essay Contest

When blind men sought to determine the nature of an elephant by feel alone, one chanced upon a leg and found an elephant to be very like a tree. Experience must be evaluated carefully. And, certainly September 11th, 2001 was a powerful experience for America.

I have many reactions. I am filled with remorse for the victims, admiration for the rescuers, and awe for the rebuilders. The passengers on United Flight 93 who fought the hijackers to a fiery death deserve a Congressional Medal of Honor as much as anyone ever did. There are so many sides to the tragedy.

But, as these events fade into history, I find that I am also filled with disappointment about a major aspect of our reaction to that fateful day.

We expect that some good will come from even the greatest catastrophe. At the time, I felt certain that America would emerge with a greater feeling of empathy for those who suffer or have suffered from other catastrophes in other lands. Comparisons would be made between the families of those who were seen hurtling to their death from the upper floors of The World Trade Center and the families of that trainload of child refugees wiped out at the train station in Dresden. We would reflect upon the difference between six thousand deaths and sixty thousand deaths, and search for some perspective about it. We would try to attach some reality to the slaughter of Russian peasants, to Rwanda, to Vietnam—perhaps even to the tens of millions who died in a long-forgotten civil war in China in the 1860s.

In short, I was sure we would see some reduction in America's preoccupation with itself. Suffering would be a great leveler, I thought—a reminder that all humans are alike, that we have everything in common, that we have a history of suffering, that suffering in one country is like suffering in another, and that only an accident of birth separates me from my brother in a foreign land.

It's no small thing. About the most dangerous idea one can imagine is for us to think that we are, somehow, above or apart from the rest of humanity. It is especially important now, with our new-found economic and military dominance as the "world's only superpower." More and more, by choice or by circumstance, we are assuming the role of a de facto world government. But, to the extent that we act as the world's government, the people of the world become citizens of that government, and we inherit an awesome responsibility toward them.

Will this "government" be a government where all men and women are equal, or will it be a government run by an American elite for their own purposes? The answer will hinge on our view of the people outside our borders. Will we have a world of "we, the people," or a world of "them and us," with us on top and them in constant revolt? Certainly, some aspects of recent history are enough to cause concern, and this concern existed long before September 11th. So I did think that tragic day would serve to remind us of our bond to the rest of humanity.

But nothing of the sort has happened. Instead, America has turned even further inward. To read the millions of words written and spoken about the World Trade Center disaster, one would imagine that the event was without precedent—that such a tragedy had never occurred before. One would think that never before in the history of mankind had there been such heroism, such promising lives cut short, such evil, such psychological damage to survivors, such orphans, such widows, such smoke, such fire, such wreckage, such inspired rebuilding, such willpower.

Intellectually, of course, we know better. Other countries have suffered tragedies as great or greater, other heroes performed incredible feats there too, other survivors went insane, other outstanding citizens perished, other flames shot as high into the air, and other places were rebuilt. But emotionally, we had always

managed to stay distant from the human aspects of these events—
and perhaps there were good reasons for us to have done so.

But now it has happened here, and logically speaking, we
can only imagine our suffering to be unique if we imagine
ourselves to be unique—a race apart, somehow, from the bulk of
humanity. And that seems to me to be the most dangerous idea we
could have.

Bonfire At Night

A haven
created by chemistry,
encircled by dancing shadows.

Fire.
We hunker close, gaze into the depth,
transfixed, pondering.

Flame has a gentle touch.
It caresses, bursts, consumes.
Sticks and logs in the jumble
billow orange and yellow.
Coals glow a dozen shades of red.

A blue jet flares for a long moment
from a saw cut end of Burr Oak.
A saddle of brown bark, puffed loose,
falls, trailing sparks to the bed of coals,
and bursts into its own miniature holocaust.

Nature's art, child of her science,
on a three dimensional palette.
Colors a Picasso would die for
parade and dance—
a million ballerinas, large and small.

Our remote ancestors gazed into such flames.
Fire was food, safety, warmth and light.
Fire was life and death, fire was God,
beneficent or terrible.

John Huss was tied to a stake in Bavaria,
and burned alive.

The Polyester Grail

Even the Black Knight sought the Holy Grail, I suppose.

For us today the grail is, undoubtedly, democracy. We laud it, extol it, and seek to export it to all of mankind. So we ought to think carefully about it—what is democracy anyway? How did we get it, how do we keep it, and why doesn't everybody have it?

Questions like these have been important at least since the age of Pericles in Athens. They are especially compelling now. Violence engulfed many parts of the world as soon as they were free of the yoke of Soviet control. In Russia itself, widespread crime and hardship followed the collapse of Communism, and extremists seemed to be winning popular favor for a time, as they still seem to be doing in the Middle East and elsewhere. Some local conflicts refused to even pause to participate in the Cold War.

And here at home the racially tinged class struggle raises the nightmare of civil unrest. In the suburbs, Americans are apt to view these matters with some impatience. "The News," for them, is a tiresome round of senseless violence that exists in the world of television; it can be dealt with by simply changing the channel.

When we think about it at all, we are apt to see democracy as being characterized by majority rule. It seems simple—everybody votes, and in the long run the majority wins. In the short run, of course, minorities are protected against majority excesses by a constitution. The question of who gets to vote can be a stickler, as in Palestine, although it's usually not a major issue in the United States anymore, Gore v. Bush notwithstanding.

But many feel there are other things that characterize democracy too, such as freedom and civil rights, so a problem arises when the majority seems to support an "undemocratic" idea or candidate

Algeria is a case in point. That North African nation's proud history dates back two thousand years, but the French invaded and conquered in 1830, and Algeria became part of the French Empire. Many French people moved there; culturally, in many ways, Algiers became a French city. When I was there in 1943 it seemed to be much like Marseille. The view in France was that Algeria was part of France. Not a colony, not a possession, but a part of France as much as Texas is a part of the United States.

Others, however, saw an oppressive colonialism that had devastated their once-proud nation. They wanted to be independent of France. A bloody eight-year War of National Liberation erupted, and Algeria won its independence in 1962. Thousands of settlers fled to Europe, but France, and Algerians of French ancestry, continued to hold positions of influence in a country that was 99% Sunni Muslim.

Algeria's first government, headed by Ben Bella, was radical, authoritarian and socialistic; after three years it was overthrown by a coup, and more moderate elements gradually took over. Most of the direct influence of the French government, notably their military bases and their control of the oil industry, was finally eliminated, but democratic reforms had to wait until 1988, and then came only as the result of widespread rioting with heavy casualties. A free election was finally held in 1990.

The election was a shocker. Fundamentalist Muslims, repeating their political success in Iran, had formed a strong party, the FIS, which won surprising support at the polls. Following this success, the FIS used violent protests to push hard for reforms in the electoral process. Another election was approaching and it became apparent that, if it was held, the FIS would take over control of Algeria.

But, for many, the FIS represented a movement that held democracy in utter contempt. If they gained control the fledgling democracy would be dead. The essence of the democratic process, the free election, would have been used to kill a democracy that thousands had suffered and died for. Should a democracy be allowed to commit suicide in this way? Or should a tyrant intervene?

In Algeria the existing government, whether from motives base or noble, chose to intervene and canceled (postponed) the 1992 election. If the FIS needed a villain, it had one now. Their protests grew more violent and the result was something akin to civil war. The apparent complicity of the West in the government's action added to the indignation of the FIS and its supporters. Algiers became a dangerous place for intellectuals and for all westerners. News reporters were a special target—the New York Times once reported that, by early summer 1995, forty six journalists had been killed in Algeria.

Algeria is by no means the first place where the idea of democracy was seen to be relatively unimportant to the majority of the people. Some societies are perhaps too primitive for such an institution to have any chance of being established, or for it to work if it was. Animals don't have democracies, or need them, so the concept may have been irrelevant for the human race prior to some stage of the evolution of culture. Other countries may have been so thoroughly under the control of an oppressive regime that it was impossible for the people to even think.

But there is no need to look to prehistory for examples, or to nations of slaves. Consider Germany and Adolph Hitler.

The German nation has often been called a "nation of thinkers." In the arts, as well as in the sciences, Germany has, for centuries, epitomized the nobility of the human mind and spirit.

Nearly five hundred years ago, Luther's powerful prose, and his doctrine of "Scripture and plain reason," gave Christianity a form that could be accepted by the modern world. Luther lost much of his popular support in the aftermath of the great peasant revolt of 1524, but initially his reforms were very popular—a device by which the people were able to speak in an age when such a thing was almost unknown.

Later, German poets celebrated the inner world as the only great object of poetry. Goethe and Schiller converted the theme of poetry from an imitation of the ancients to a celebration of the ideal of humanity. Hegel conceived the state as the realization of the mind of the people. Even the brief treatise "Germania," published by Tacitus in the year 98 A.D., describes a democracy that prevailed among the Germanic tribes. *The men assembled in arms and listened to speeches by the king or military chief, indicating their dissent by loud murmurs, their approval by rattling their spears,* he says.

The abdication of the Emperor and the collapse of his whole imperial regime after World War I seemed to open the way for communism, but the bureaucrats stayed at their posts and a provisional government was able to avert civil war and set up elections for a constitutional democracy. Happy Day! More than thirty million Germans went to the polls, and the Weimar Republic was born.

We all know the rest. That government, under intense pressure from extremists on both the left and the right, was also burdened with impossible demands by the Treaty of Versailles. World depression came in 1929. It caused great hardship in Germany, and the republic was made captive by the extreme right, bringing Hitler to power in 1933.

A remarkable thing about the Nazi regime is the short time it lasted—only twelve years. By 1945, Hitler was history. Some seventy million people had died as a result of the German people's experiment in government, including more than ten million murdered in Hitler's death camps, some sixty percent of them Jews.

The military and industrial accomplishments of Germany during WWII would be awe-inspiring if they had not been put to such gruesome and evil ends. How could such a small country do all of this?

The question is one that should haunt every proponent of democracy. The short answer is that most Germans accepted Hitler's ambitions as their own, and then did their best, physically and mentally, to bring those ambitions to fruition. No sacrifice was too great. German battle losses and civilian casualties were astronomical while industrial production soared, even in the face of massive and continuous aerial bombardment.

The misbegotten accomplishments of those people could not have come from a top-driven society. Things like this require initiative at all levels. Perhaps Hitler wasn't even the real instigator. Perhaps the ambitions originated with the people; and it was Hitler who did the accepting?

But why did the people of this culturally advanced nation give up their freedom and their democracy in favor of a ruthless quest for power as cogs in a well-oiled terror machine?

Is mankind's thirst for freedom really the all-consuming passion that we imagine it to be; or is this idea merely a rationalization that hides more shallow motives? Is it really freedom that the slave seeks, or is it simply power and affluence? The huddled masses may yearn to be free, but that really proves nothing. What do the affluent yearn for? How free are they in our conformist society, and what use do they make of the freedom they have? Is our grail, democracy, something holy and golden, something to live for and die for, or is it merely useful for the moment—something we will support as long as it feeds us and clothes us so magnificently? Is our grail actually made of polyester?

At the close of World War II, one question was on the minds of most Americans as they looked at the wreckage of Germany. The question has been largely forgotten now, but it was an agonizing one then. We looked back at the short history of the Hitler era and wondered—could what took place in Germany have happened in America?

Germany and the United States were, as countries go, alike in many respects—centers of industrial might, worshippers of technology. At the end of World War II, when U.S. troops occupied Germany, I remember well that a common sentiment among my fellow soldiers was that it was really nice to finally be in a place that was more like home. Our government found it necessary to publish articles that attempted to indoctrinate us. We should not, one article said, allow our mutual admiration for a sit-down toilet that flushes to blind us to the reasons that Germany was our enemy and France was our friend.

But the GIs of that era were largely immune to such advice from their government. Contrary to today's popular view of what it was like then, we didn't really believe in much of anything. The extent to which World War II has already become mythologized is remarkable.

A major feature of U.S. policy toward occupied Germany at that time was the edict of "Non-fraternization." It was a big deal, but a measure of the gap that existed between the government's theory and the GI's reception of it may be inferred from the fact that most soldiers were surprised if they happened to learn that the policy applied to all Germans, and not just to the girls (with whom they actually managed to fraternize very freely). Bill Clinton, as one of his last official acts, granted a presidential pardon to a New York man, an American WWII soldier who had been court martialed and convicted of fraternization for visiting with a German woman who took in laundry. It was the only actual case that I'd ever heard of.

By the time I returned to Germany in 1952, the non-fraternization policy had been long forgotten. The relationship between the German populace and the American troops was close and friendly. We reminisced about the war with the German veterans as freely as we did among ourselves.

Could an episode like the German's embrace of fascism ever take place in America? With our present great affluence such an idea seems outlandish, but times can change. In a time of great stress, is there anything about America that would make us act in a different way than Germany did?

Perhaps there is no reasonable likelihood that our devotion to democracy will ever be subjected to such a great stress. But some unsettling things have happened in America in recent years. We hear again and again that the gap between rich and poor is widening. Also that poverty is visited disproportionately on blacks and other minorities. To some extent, these people live in a separate world from the rest of us—a grim world where children grow up without families, without education, without guidance, without role models. The "War on Drugs" is a daily terror for them; crime is commonplace. Children even go armed to school and shoot each other. At home they eke out an existence among drugged and drunk adults who routinely ignore or abuse them.

We hear also that these children grow up with no faith in America's systems of justice. They populate our prisons until the walls are ready to burst, and lawbreakers are popular heroes, often even among their victims. And we hear that they are organizing, in a way. The antisocial gang has become the social unit that many of them build their lives around. It is, they claim, the only place where they have a place—their only refuge of dignity. America's first response to this problem was a flight to the suburbs. This tactic is being carried a step further now—walled communities have become popular—private cities with armed guards who allow no one to enter who doesn't have business there.

These are ominous trends—two worlds forming armed camps, with an escalating rhetoric of violence.

Politically, our response at the moment has been a decided shift to the right. Crime prevention programs, derided as "midnight basketball," have been drastically cut in favor of longer sentences and bigger prisons, and tax policy favors measures that further widen the gap between rich and poor. So our society is under some stress, and it may grow worse.

These flaws in our social system are of great concern, and worthy of every effort to repair them, but that doesn't necessarily mean that they threaten democracy here. Social injustice is nothing new, and it doesn't always lead to revolution or to a dictatorship. Criminal justice and penal codes in other countries have been far more barbaric than in ours, if equally ineffective. All felonies were punished by death in England two centuries ago, and hangings were public celebrations, but democracy prevailed anyway.

Still—the past is not always a reliable guide to the future. It may be that our social problems will eventually threaten democracy itself. No one can say. What puzzles me is whether anyone would really care. Is democracy, as such, any more important to us than it is to the Algerians or was to the Germans? Or is it something that is only important because of the material things that seem to flow from it? Unless and until a crisis of great proportions arises, we will probably never know.

But I fear that a great deal of America's supposed worship of freedom arises from hype and harangue. My guess is that, in dire circumstances, we might wave goodbye to democracy as readily and as thoughtlessly as the Germans did.

At the Oasis

At the Oasis, democracy is not accorded a free ride. Like everything else, it has to prove itself anew with each passing day, or at least whenever the subject comes up. When Sam says that the Japs had good beer, that's one for the Japs. Or, as Sam would no doubt have put it, the goddamn Japs. It's left to Budweiser and Coors to measure up on their own merits if they can.

Most of the denizens of the stools at the Oasis are fans of the Minnesota Vikings and the Minnesota Twins, and come to each new season with high hopes for these home teams. But loyalty does not imply blind support—in fact, most of the discussion centers on perceived faults in the home team's players, owners, and coaches. Rarely do I hear anything good about any of them. The depth of these criticisms always amazes me. If these guys really know as much about football as they seem to, then I am indeed a dunce by comparison. But even if they actually don't know so much about it, and even if (perish the thought) there is really not all that much to know about it, I'm always pleased to hear their talk. The talk seems to me to speak of a world where man is not simply a pawn in the hands of some impersonal fate. These guys are so involved in the world that they force the world to pay attention to them. In sum, over the country, late or soon, on topics trivial or crucial, these discussions come to be heard and heeded. And that's what keeps the country going.

It's hard to put into words any specific vision of what we hope the future will bring. Each aspect of that world depends upon so many others. If fusion research finally succeeds, and energy becomes incomparably cheaper, cleaner, and more plentiful, then our ideas about limiting population, which seem so vital now, may all be overturned. To limit population is to deny life to billions of unborn people, so it's a vital question, it seems to me. Other types of new science could also lead to a life that is very different from the one we know. Nanotechnology envisions a world where vastly improved jet engines can be grown like watermelons instead of being painstakingly assembled from hundreds or thousands of manufactured parts. Biotechnology can already clone sheep and modify plants. We are, in all probability, much closer to the beginning of this age of technology than to the end of it, so it is hard for us to even imagine the world that our great grandchildren and their descendants will live in. Earth-shaking decisions will have to be made about questions that we don't yet know enough to even ask.

So I hope that the Oasis, and thousands of places like it, will still be there to kick these ideas around as they arise. It will need help, it is true, lots of help from think tanks, research laboratories, congress, and the United Nations, among others, but agencies like these can go awry without the continuing and detailed nit picking that we provide. The world may change, but the Oasis will be, I hope, eternal.

Eternal as an institution, that is. We as individuals, and even our stools at the counter and our spot along the road, will certainly pass and be forgotten. I am acutely conscious of this inevitable fact as I write. My friend, Sam, of whom I spoke so often in earlier chapters, has recently died. We mourn his passing, of course, and we will miss him sorely, but we celebrate his life too. Sam, during his life, did meritorious things as a son, a brother, a husband, a father, a worker and a soldier. But I will always remember him best for his searching and irascible comments on the passing scene over so many breakfasts At the Oasis.

About the Author

Bill McDonald was born on a farm near Nunda, South Dakota, in 1924. After a childhood on such farms and in one-room country schools, he served in the U.S. Army in Africa and Europe during World War II, and then took advantage of the GI Bill to attend college, graduating with a double major in physics and mathematics. He married a local girl; they raised four children who are now raising children of their own.

Bill has juggled careers—in industry, as an industrial physicist; in the military, as a now retired reserve colonel; in agriculture, as a lifetime part time farmer; and in local government. In addition, he attended law school late in life and was admitted to the Minnesota Bar in 1982, practicing primarily in Family Court, Juvenile Court, and as a Guardian ad Litem for juveniles. More recently, he returned to school and earned a master of fine arts degree in English, with a specialty in creative writing, from Mankato State University in 1995.

His previous publications include scientific papers as well as *Dakota Incarnate*, a collection of short stories published by New Rivers Press in 1999, and *The Nunda Irish*, a 1991 self published fictionalized history of a Dakota community. Dakota Incarnate was a 1997 Minnesota Voices competition winner. He has also published a number of poems, short stories, and essays in various literary journals. His poem, "A Cosmic Villanelle," was nominated for the Pushcart Prize XXV anthology in 1999.

ISBN 141206810-X